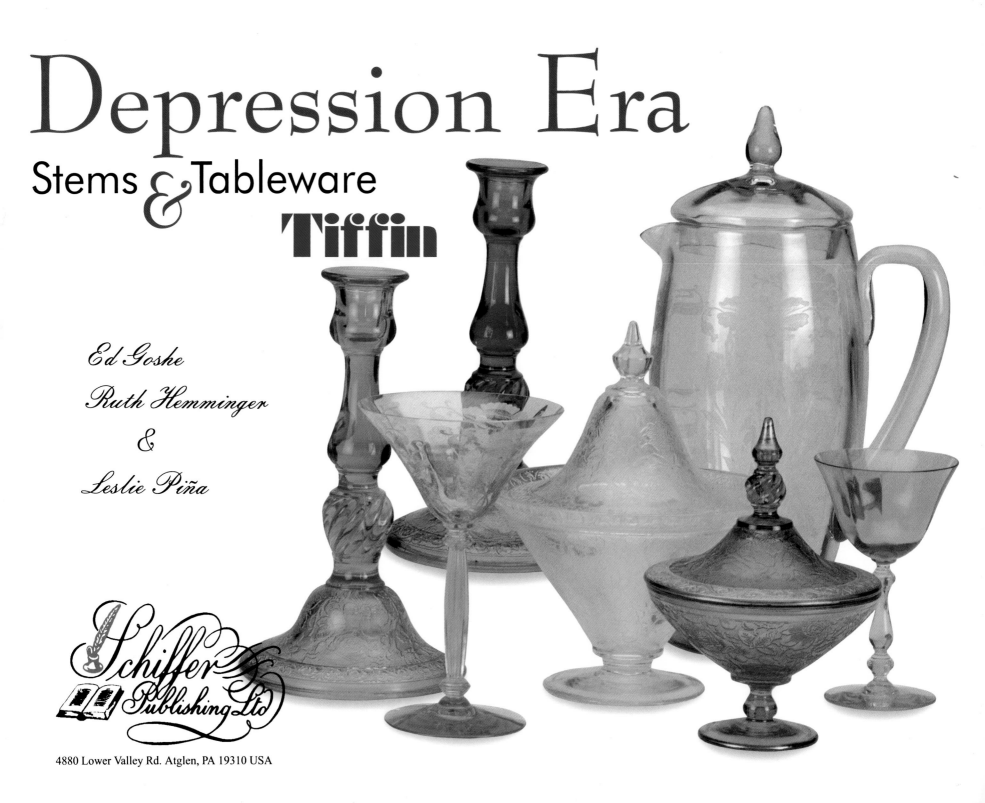

Depression Era
Stems & Tableware
Tiffin

Ed Goshe

Ruth Hemminger

&

Leslie Piña

Schiffer Publishing Ltd

4880 Lower Valley Rd. Atglen, PA 19310 USA

Designed by Leslie Piña
Layout by Bonnie M. Hensley
Typeset in Zurich BT

ISBN: 0-7643-0652-9
Printed in China
1 2 3 4

Published by Schiffer Publishing Ltd.
4880 Lower Valley Road
Atglen, PA 19310
Phone: (610) 593-1777; Fax: (610) 593-2002
E-mail: Schifferbk@aol.com
Please write for a free catalog.
This book may be purchased from the publisher.
Please include $3.95 for shipping.

In Europe, Schiffer books are distributed by
Bushwood Books
6 Marksbury Avenue
Kew Gardens
Surrey TW9 3BQ England
Phone: 44 (0)181 392-8585; Fax: 44 (0)181 392-9876
E-mail: Bushwd@aol.com

Please try your bookstore first.
We are interested in hearing from authors
with book ideas on related subjects.

Contents

Credits

The desire to capture this beautiful stemware and tableware in color led us, as collectors and admirers of Tiffin Glass, to this attempt to document many of our favorite Tiffin patterns. Because of the large number of etchings and engravings in several colors, sometimes on several stemlines, it is virtually impossible to gather them all in one volume. This book focuses on tableware produced from 1914-1940 and includes most of the popular patterns, as well as many obscure designs. To make this volume as comprehensive as possible, we were aided by the following people with the loan of their glassware: Eddie Beisner, Howard and Janet Beisner, Dale and Eunice Cover, Janet A. Dell, The Gallery -- Richard and Beverly Digby, Char and Dave Distel, Richard and Virginia Distel, Gary C. and Jan L. Dundore, Jon Eakin (Gerald Eakin collection), Paul and Nellie Haugh, Leanne Wolff-Langenderfer, Precious and Few -- Dee and Tony Mondloch, Fr. Frank Murd, Robert and Donna Overholt, Bill Reyer, Harold and Betty Scherger, Suzanne Smith and Paul J. Williams.

We are grateful to those who assisted us at libraries and other public institutions, especially Carolyn Goshe and Bill Reyer for helping research the files at Carnegie Library of Pittsburgh, Pennsylvania; the Cleveland Public Library, Cleveland, Ohio; and Rosalie Adams, Director of the Seneca County Museum, for the loan of the glassworkers photograph, etchings and other valuable information. Thanks also to John Bing for his computer drawings and his help in preparing the manuscript. Finally, thanks to Ramon Piña and Lyman Hemminger for their assistance at all of the photo sessions and for their moral support during this project.

Preface

Although there is no doubt among collectors as to what Depression era glass is, there can be some confusion regarding its terminology. The period in American history known as the Great Depression began immediately after the stock market crash of 1929 and ended about when World War II began. Of course the "end" was not abrupt like the beginning, and the decade of the 1930s is referred to as the Depression era.

During the Depression and later, a specific and easily recognizable type of inexpensive pressed glass was produced by a number of companies. It was usually made into tableware in one of several soft pastel colors, and it sold for pennies. Sets were popular in retail stores, and pieces were used as premiums to promote other products. My grandfather had two movie theaters in Cleveland, Ohio in the late 1930s and early 1940s, and he gave pieces of Depression glass to moviegoers. The glass was popular, because the idea to make large quantities of inexpensive glass was a good one. It provided color and imitated the elegance of dinner tables that many Americans could not afford. Pretty colors and patterns were more important than the fact that it was not made, decorated, or finished by hand. The cheapness of what has come to be called Depression glass was a major reason for its success, but when it began to intrigue collectors, it ceased to be inexpensive.

Not all Depression glass was made during the Depression, and certainly not all glass produced during the Depression is Depression glass. Another major category is known as Depression era glass. It has also been called "elegant" or "classic," and a number of other equally imprecise and arbitrary names. Dictionary definitions of the term elegant include words like "refined, tasteful, luxurious, dignified," and "graceful." It is also defined as "polished." Now, in this definition, polish refers to manners, but the process of polishing glass to provide a finish is also one of the distinguishing characteristics of Depression era glass. Where Depression glass was left unpolished, the so-called elegant Depression era glass was given a fine finish by methods using fire, acid, or abrasion.

These finishing techniques, and production methods in general, in large well-organized glass factories had become very efficient by the 1930s. Many people who had become accustomed to using a higher quality glassware continued to use it for gifts and to set their tables. These glassware buyers also represented a sizable market, and demand for fine blown and molded glassware was high enough to support the major factories, all located in the tri-state area of Ohio, West Virginia, and Pennsylvania. One of the largest and longest running of these factories was Fostoria, which began in northwestern Ohio, only to move to Moundsville, West Virginia, within a few years. But no more than a few miles from Fostoria, Ohio was, and still is, the town of Tiffin. Beginning in 1914, the Tiffin Glass factory expanded into producing fine blown and molded stemware and tableware in countless patterns. By the 1930s, the "Depression era," the output and variety were impressive.

The variety will be enough to keep diligent collectors busy into the twenty-first century. For example, one line or one pattern of just stemware is apt to include six or even eight different stems, from big water goblets to little cordials. A line might be made in four or five different colors and combinations, such as crystal bowl and colored stem or the reverse. That means that there could easily be forty different items in one stem line before any decoration is added. With choices like etchings, cuttings, optics, and gold bands, the line may have had another four or five different decorations added, bringing the number of possible distinctly different, identifiable, and collectible items in one stem line to about 200! Multiply this by dozens of major lines, and it becomes apparent how complex the output of one glass factory would have been. If there were about a dozen of these major companies plus many more smaller ones, then the variety of glassware produced, even in one decade, is mind-boggling. And all of these varied design lines, colors, and decorations are collectively referred to as "Depression era" glass. In addition, there was probably as much Depression era glass made after the Depression as there was in the 1930s.

This book represents only a small sample of Depression era glass, but it is an extraordinary sample, because Tiffin was one extraordinary glass company. Factory production during the Depression was fairly well documented and enough to keep any collector occupied for years. Most of the glass presented in this volume is from the 1920s and 1930s. Our goal is to provide a guide to help the collector, researcher, and dealer identify, price, and enjoy this compelling glassware. As avid collectors and researchers of Tiffin Glass for many years, as well as leaders of the Tiffin Glass Collectors, Ed Goshe and Ruth Hemminger are well suited for this task. My interests are less focused, covering many other categories of twentieth-century decorative arts as well. But as this Tiffin project evolved and grew, I realized how significant a contribution Tiffin had made to the history of American glassmaking and to the history of decorative arts and material culture. We hope that the readers will share our appreciation and joy in experiencing these little historic documents and works of art.

Leslie Piña
February, 1998

A Tribute to the Glassworkers of Factory R

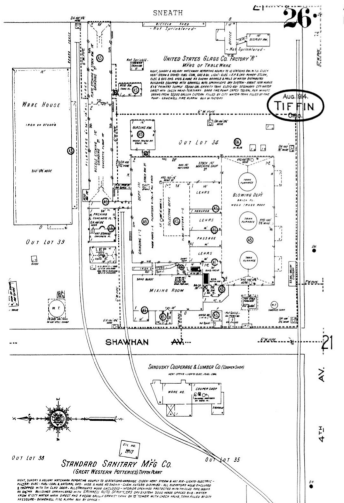

August 1914 floor plan of Factory R.

In July, 1888, it was announced that the A.J. Beatty and Sons glass factory of Steubenville, Ohio, would be relocating in Tiffin, Ohio. A.J. Beatty had been negotiating with various communities for more than a year to establish a site for their new factory. The city of Tiffin offered five years of natural gas, $35,000 in cash, and land valued at $15,000. Construction of a three-furnace glass factory at the corner of Fourth Avenue and Vine Street began in September, 1888, and operations commenced on August 15, 1889. Early production capacity was reported to be 500,000 pressed tumblers per week.

A Tribute to the Glassworkers of Factory R This 1936 photo includes only a few of the men and women who labored over the years to produce the beautiful tableware that carried the Tiffin name. The efforts of thousands of faithful employees resulted in a thriving and profitable glass industry that survived in Tiffin, Ohio, for over nine decades. Tiffin Glass collectors everywhere owe a debt of gratitude to all of the glassworkers for their achievements. They produced some of the finest glassware in the world.

1936 Factory R workers: (Seated Left to Right) **Row 1** - Neil Funkhauser, Harold Barnhart, Howard Lang, Unknown, Henry "Heinie" Definbaugh, Ralford Sours, Ray Carry, Unknown, Mr. Mantz, Ray Tally, Alford Malherby, Mr. Glick, Joseph Stiener, Harmon Rohe, Cliff Gardner, Claude Meese, Unknown, Jake Ferstler, Clem Heck, Raleigh Meyers, Voris Banks, Audrey Doll, Hugo Wall, Mike Ferstler, Kelly Decker, Walt Foncannon, Don West. **Row 2** - "Red" Drew, Charles Long, Ray Dryfuse, Ralph Ringle, Unknown, Herman Fey, Francis Mitchell, Carl Heck, Jim DelTurco, Unknown, Unknown, Unknown, Unknown, Al Krupp, Earl Shuman, Jim Turner, Joe Fey, Billy Shoupe, Charles Elchert, Unknown, Archie Kahler, Rusty Swartz, John Rarick, Jim Collier, Lucian Delvenne, Mr. Mestry, Ernest Ferstler, John Cronin. **Row 3** - Jerry Kinn, Unknown, Mr. Funkhauser, Billy Auger, Evert Wall, Vincent Bentz, Lester Rohe, Paul Kastner, Walt Asman, John Dutt, Roy Williams, Unknown, Ben Nevius, "Dog" Badgent, Art Kloupp, Eldon Nusbaum, Mr. Alfords, Joseph Bernard, Ben Porter, Hank Rahrig, John Slottermiller. **Row 4** - Mr. Grieselding, Carl Theander, Charles Hayward, Harold Bour, Charles Kirchner, Paul Rohe, "Shorty" Long, Hank Ranker, Herman Kirian, Lewis Ranker, Oscar Bernard, George "Toots" Turner, Frank Hahler, Jon Wagner, "Slim" Jenkins, George Miller, Joe Lambert, Leonard Emmons, Jerald Malherby, Unknown, Carmon DelTurco, Casper Sours, Paul Williams, Ralph Bender, "Fritz" Herrik, Carl Runion, Harold Peck, George Kastner, Pete Ferstler, Paul Everhart, Alvin Bame, Frank Turner, Tom Burkhart.

A.J. Beatty and Sons merged with the United States Glass Company on January 1, 1892, and became one of nineteen factories of the large corporation. The Tiffin factory was designated Factory R. On May 23, 1893, less than two years later, Factory R was destroyed by fire. The factory was rebuilt in Tiffin in return for two additional years of free natural gas.

During the early years of the 1900s, there was a gradual shift from pressed to blown tableware, in response to customers' demands. Needle etchings, plate etchings, engravings, and sand blast designs were applied to the new blown tableware. The glass items were identified by a paper label with the letters USG intertwined within a gold-colored shield. Commercial ware continued to be marketed under the United States Glass Company name until September, 1927. After that time household goods were identified by a gold paper label with TIFFIN superimposed over a large "T" within a shield.

Prior to the mid 1920s, production of tableware at Factory R was primarily in Crystal. With the increase in popularity of colored glassware, the United States Glass Company began the production of a variety of pastel colors, and darker shades, including Rose Pink, Reflex Green, Sky Blue, Mandarin, Lilac, Twilite, Canary, Emerald Green, Amber, Ruby, Amethyst, Amberina, Royal Blue, Old Gold, and Black. A satin finish was sometimes applied to tableware during the 1920s and 1930s. Stemware and tableware remained the primary output of Factory R during this time.

While other factories within the United States Glass Company were forced to close during the Great Depression of the 1930s, Factory R managed to survive. In 1937, the offices of the United States Glass Company were transferred from Pittsburgh to Tiffin with C.W. Carlson as President. By 1940, all glassware was marked with a Tiffin label; however, the official name of the company remained as the United States Glass Company through 1962.

In the 1940s, three major changes took place in the use of tableware by the American public resulting in a transition of Tiffin's production. Crystal stemware regained its popularity over colored stemware, and fewer items were produced in each stemline. Also to a large degree, china replaced the use of glass tableware for table settings.

Although the focus of Tiffin's production continued to be stemware, a new line of Modern designs contributed to the prosperity of the Tiffin factory. The introduction, under the direction of Mr. Carlson, of the Swedish Modern line, later renamed Tiffin Modern in May, 1946, was the beginning of the production of Tiffin's famous heavy offhand shapes. Interest in Modern free-form designs continued into the 1960s.

When Mr. Carlson retired in 1959, the company was struggling for survival because of overwhelming competition from inexpensive imported glassware. The factory was sold to a New York investment firm in 1959, but remained known as the United States Glass Company. Bankruptcy occurred in 1962, and the factory closed for a few months. Four former employees bought the plant in 1963, and renamed it the Tiffin Art Glass Company. This transaction marked the end of the United States Glass Company. Business improved, but on June 4, 1966, the company was again sold, this time to a major corporation, the Continental Can Company. It was renamed the Tiffin Glass Company, Inc. During these years, stemware remained the major focus of production, with blown and pressed ware also manufactured.

The factory changed hands again when it was purchased in December, 1968, by another large corporation, Interpace, the parent company of Franciscan China. On May 10, 1979, the factory was sold for the last time to Towle Silversmiths. The furnaces were shut down on May 1, 1980, the date considered by collectors to be the end of the Tiffin Glass Company. The Outlet Store and a decorating shop remained open until October, 1984, when the facility permanently closed.

Throughout Tiffin's history, the quality of the company's fine stemware remained the foundation for the success of this leading glassmaking firm. From 1914 through 1980, the Tiffin factory produced thousands of patterns on hundreds of stemlines and remained competitive with other major tableware manufacturers. Many of the designs continue to be favorites with Tiffin Glass enthusiasts today.

Introduction

In 1927, the term Tiffinware was introduced by the United States Glass Company in a marketing campaign to advertise glassware produced from all the United States Glass Company factories. This decision was made to capitalize on the success of the Tiffin name, which resulted from the popularity of the company's fine blown stemware produced at Factory R, Tiffin, Ohio.

The focus of the contents of this book is the glassware produced at Factory R of the United States Glass Company from 1914-1940. Some of the tableware included in this volume was produced at Factory G, Glassport, Pennsylvania, and Factory K located in Pittsburgh, Pennsylvania, and is considered Tiffinware, as are all of the products of Factory R.

Company terminology is used in the captions to describe items. Today, some of these older terms have been replaced with modern nomenclature; for example, sundaes are now referred to as sherbets, seltzers as juices, jugs as pitchers, table tumblers as waters, and comports as compotes. Company line numbers usually consisted of a five digit number, i.e. #15024; however, some catalog pages reference only the final three digits, i.e. #024. To be consistent, we have used the five digit line numbers, when known.

Color names varied over the years. Rose Pink was sometimes simply referred to as Rose, Reflex Green as Apple Green, and Mandarin as Topaz. Green trim could be Green, Reflex Green, or Nile Green. In addition, early color shades were not always consistent. The Rose Pink color varied from a soft pastel pink to an orange-pink tint, and Twilite ranged from pale lavender to blue. This early Twilite color differs in spelling and color from the lavender color Twilight produced in the 1950s through the 1970s at the Tiffin factory.

A stemline number is determined by the combination of the shape of the bowl and the shape of the stem. The same stem, with a different shaped bowl would indicate a different stemline number. When describing two-tone objects, the predominant color is listed first, with the trim color following. The term "trim" refers to an additional color applied to the body of a glass object. For example, a Crystal goblet with Green trim indicates a Crystal bowl with an applied Green stem and foot.

A complete plate etching or engraving may not always appear on some stemware. Large patterns were sometimes reduced in size to fit on a smaller bowl. An example is the Luciana etching. The complete etching includes three figurals. It was reduced to include only two figures on the smaller stemware items.

In photo captions, object, color and optic names are capitalized. The dimensions are measured at the widest point. An "h." indicates that the height is the largest dimension of the object. Names or phrases found within double quotations marks are not United States Glass Company terms, but are names or phrases adopted by the authors or are generally used by collectors.

Prices are listed in U.S. dollars at the end of the caption. Each item is priced using a value range. These values were derived from actual purchase prices, by prices seen at antiques shows or shops, or by rarity and desirability. The prices are listed in the order in which the respective pieces appear in the photo. These values are intended as a guide, and neither the authors nor the publisher are responsible for any transactions based on this guide.

Glassmaking Terms

The following definitions are general glassmaking terms that apply to references used within this volume.

Blank. An undecorated glass object.

Blown Glass. Glass objects produced by the forcing of air by a glassworker through a blowpipe into molten glass.

Cased Glass. A glass object formed by applying a layer of glass over a contrasting color.

Crimped. The result of shaping the rim of a glass object into a scalloped edge.

Crystal. Clear or colorless glass.

Cutting. 1. A general term which describes the process of applying a design to a glass surface by the contact of the object against a rotating wheel. 2. The design or pattern which has been applied to a glass object.

Emery Cut. Another term for sand blast.

Engraving. Another term for cutting a design on a glass object.

Gray Cutting. An engraving that has not been hand or acid polished.

Iridescent Glass. Glass with a rainbow-like appearance created by applying a coating to achieve a lustrous effect.

Line. A distinct design of glassware.

Needle Etching. A symmetrical design applied to glassware by machine-driven steel needles.

Optics. A series of lines, circles or patterns within the body of a glass object which are formed by the use of tools or molds.

Plate Etching. A decoration applied to glassware by a process using a flat steel plate, ink, wax, and hydrofluoric acid.

Pressed Glass. Glassware that is formed by hand or machine using a plunger to compress molten glass in a mold.

Rock Crystal. Glassware that has been cut, then dipped in acid to achieve a shiny finish.

Sand Blast. A process of etching a design in glassware using sand and air pressure directed over a metal shield.

Tableware. Items other than stemware with the same design or pattern.

Identification Guide

Optics

Optics used in stemware are a series of lines or patterns which are formed by the use of tools or molds. Eleven different optics were used in the manufacture of Tiffin stemware. Wide optic, sometimes referred to as Regular optic, was the most common. Some stemware lines were made without optic. Tiffin discontinued use of most of these optics in the 1930s; they continued to use the Wide and Havana optics in later stemware production. Other glass companies used many of these same optics; however, they did not always identify them by the Tiffin Glass optic names.

Gold and Platinum Bands

Gold or platinum was applied to etched bands used to decorate many different shapes of stemware and tableware throughout the production years of Tiffin Glass. Twenty-four karat gold was used. The Minton, Rambler Rose, Laurel and Valencia bands were used by other glass and china companies as well.

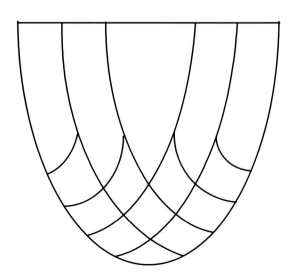

Block

This September 20, 1926 advertisement from *China, Glass, and Lamps* lists the optics available from the United States Glass Company. At the present time the Chain and Radiant optics remain unidentified.

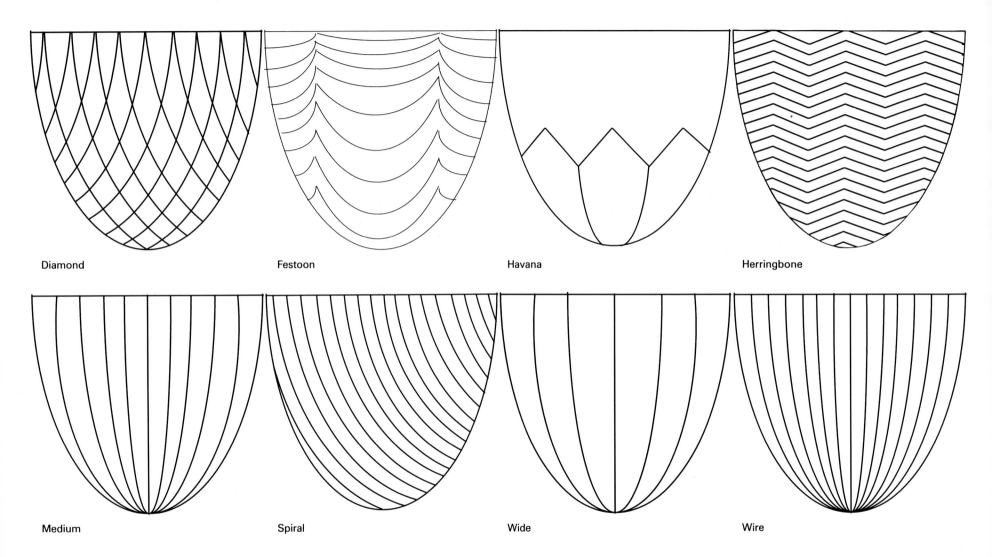

Diamond

Festoon

Havana

Herringbone

Medium

Spiral

Wide

Wire

12

Gold and Platinum Bands

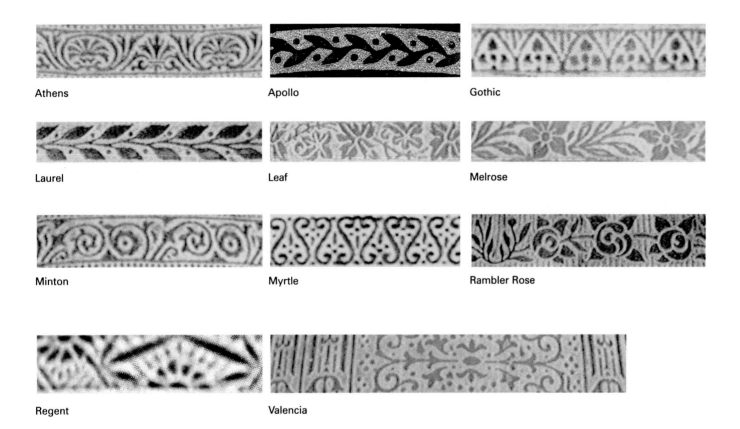

Athens

Apollo

Gothic

Laurel

Leaf

Melrose

Minton

Myrtle

Rambler Rose

Regent

Valencia

13

Chapter 1: Needle Etchings

Needle

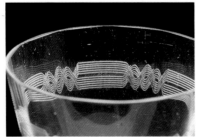

The symmetrical designs of needle etching were popular United States Glass Company offerings from c. 1911 through 1940. Numerous designs were available on Crystal, Rose Pink or Green blanks. Needle etched designs have gradually lost favor over the years, and they are not avidly sought after by collectors today.

From *The Glass Outlook,* September, 1924

The next time a prospective buyer asks, "How do they put these fine symmetrical designs on glassware," this can be your answer.

This is what is termed needle etching. While comparatively simple and inexpensive it adds much to the beauty of glassware.

The glass to receive the design is first thoroughly cleaned and dried. It is then placed in a wire holder and dipped in melted wax. The entire surface must be well covered and any spot not covered by the dip must be painted with a brush dipped in wax.

After the wax has hardened, the waxed glass is placed on a very intricate little motor driven machine which operates a series of steel needles that move up and down as the glass slowly revolves, cutting the same design in the wax that is to appear on the finished etched glass.

The glassware is next placed in racks and lowered into an etching solution the active element of which is hydrofluoric acid. This eats away the glass where the design has been cut into the wax.

After a certain time has elapsed the glass is taken out of the etching bath and washed in water to remove the acid. A steaming hot water bath next removes the wax and leaves the glassware, neatly polished, ready for final inspection. After polishing, the glassware is ready for packing for delivery to the customer.

Many beautiful symmetrical designs can be applied by this method and until the fairly recent development of the more expensive plate etching process, needle etched ware had only cut glass as a competitor. Even today needle etched ware is the least expensive of the etched and cut ware and for that reason alone comes into very general use in homes, hotels, clubs, and the like."

Left: Green #14188, Goblet, Wide Optic with unknown needle etching. $20-30
Top center: Crystal with Blue trim: #14185, Ice Tea; #14194, 2 qt. Jug with cover. Both Wide Optic, unknown needle etching. $15-25, $200-250
Bottom center: Detail of needle etching.

FACTORY "R," TIFFIN, OHIO.
United States Glass Company, Pittsburgh, Pa., U. S. A.
NEEDLE ETCHED.

Each design furnished on a complete line of Stemware, Tumblers, Jugs and other items.

14196. 9 oz. Goblet
Wide Optic
N/E 257

14153. 10 oz. Goblet
N/E 259

14153. 9 oz. Goblet
Wide Optic
N/E 275

14186. 9½ oz. Goblet
Wide Optic
N/E 277

14194. 9 oz. Goblet
Wide Optic
N/E 278

14198. 10 oz. Goblet
Wide Optic
N/E 279

14199. 10½ oz. Goblet
N/E 281

13630. 9 oz. Goblet
Wide Optic
N/E 305

14196. Sau Champ
Wide Optic
N/E 257

14153. Sau Champ
N/E 259

14153. Sau Champ
Wide Optic
N/E 275

14186. Sau Champ
Wide Optic
N/E 277

14194. Sau Champ
Wide Optic
N/E 278

14198. Sau Champ
Wide Optic
N/E 279

14199. Sau Champ
N/E 281

13630. Sau Champ
Wide Optic
N/E 305

Plate 1433-A

Catalog page illustrating examples of needle etchings. c. 1920.

15

Chapter 2: Plate Etchings

Plate etchings appeared on United States Glass Company stemware as early as 1913 and remained favorites with consumers into the 1940s. Some patterns were available as late as the 1970s. The etchings chosen for this volume include popular patterns produced from 1914 to 1940.

From *The Glass Outlook,* November, 1924

Wherever glassware of the better grade is stocked, you will find plate etched samples, made by the process described here. For delicacy and beauty it acknowledges no equal. In its production it calls forth all the skill of the artisans who specialize in its making. The process lends itself to the reproduction of designs that could not be produced upon glass by any other method, and enables the designer to get away entirely from the stereotyped symmetrical designs of the needle-etch process.

After a design has been selected as suitable for decoration, the first step in the process is the making of a flat steel plate on which the design stands out in fine steel lines against a depressed background etched deep into the metal. This is the master plate. In use, it is covered with a sticky black compound called the ink or resist, owing to its ability to resist the action of the etching acid. After the ink has been applied, the plate is scraped over the design with a flat bladed tool somewhat on the order of a large putty knife to remove all the resist except that which is in the deep etched out places in the plate. A piece of thin tissue paper is laid on the plate and rubbed in close contact with all parts of the design. When pulled away the paper carries the resist with it, the design showing in white against the black background.

The paper is then pressed by hand into contact with the glassware which has been cleaned previously of all foreign matter. The paper is then released by means of a solution, leaving the design transferred onto the glass. The part of the glass not covered with resist and not a part of the design, including the inside of all hollow pieces is then painted with wax, or paraffin, which after cooling also forms a resist.

The hydrofluoric acid etch is next applied to all parts of the glass not covered by the resist. This etches or eats the design into the glass, but since the acid mix is of a peculiar character, the etched lines do not become dull, but retain all the original brilliancy of the glass and appear to stand out against the clear glass background.

After the acid dip, the glassware is washed to remove all traces of acid and then immersed in steaming hot water to remove the wax and resist.

The process just described produces a clear design on clear glass. Sometimes a double etch process is used to heighten the effectiveness of [a] certain design. This calls for an entirely different acid mix applied to certain portions of the glass around the design to produce a dull etched surface as a background for the more brilliant line etching. This work calls for artistic skill of the highest degree and costs considerably more to produce than most other types of glassware decoration. That the results justify the cost, however, is proved by its increasing popularity with the discriminating public.

Authors' note: The double etch process described in the paragraph above was used to decorate a number of Tiffin stemlines. Etchings that appear with this frosted background include Adam, Arcadian, Classic, Nymph, Psyche, Luciana, Isabella, Poppy, Roses, Waterlily, and Forsythe.

Adam
Adam is one of three etchings featuring baskets. This pattern was produced in many items in Crystal from 1913-1934 on the #14178 stemline. The #33 vase is the only item documented in Amber.

Arcadian
This basket motif etching is often confused with the Adam etching. Arcadian is found on the #15030 stemline in Crystal with Green trim and the #15024 stemline in Rose Pink with Crystal trim.

Aster
A floral etched pattern produced in Crystal on stemline #13628 from 1913 through the early 1920s. Aster was also utilized on several sizes of vases.

Berian
Berian is an early 1930s etching which was produced on stemline #15074 in Crystal and Crystal with Green trim. The #15074 stemline was also produced in the late 1940s in the Killarney color.

Bridal

This 1930s etching was produced in Crystal, on the #15073 stemline, with and without a platinum band.

Byzantine

Byzantine was produced on three stemlines in the following colors: Crystal: #15037, #15040, #15048; Mandarin with Crystal trim, #15037; Crystal with Black trim, #15037; Rose Pink with Crystal trim, #15037; Mandarin with Black trim, #15037. The #15048 stemline was also decorated with a platinum Leaf band. The #8814 plate, #8177 Centerpiece bowl, and the #101 candleholders were produced in Black, with and without gold inlay.

Cadena

Cadena's leafy etching is similar in appearance to Byzantine. This pattern was produced on the #15065 stemline in Crystal, Mandarin with Crystal trim, and Rose Pink with Crystal trim. The third color combination is considered scarce. This unusual spiny stemline was used only for the Cadena etching. The Cadena etching was offered in six items in the Montgomery Ward Fall/Winter 1931-1932 catalog under their name, Queen Elizabeth Ruff, in the colors Crystal, Mandarin Gold, and Shell Pink.

Capri

A lesser known etching which was produced in Crystal on stemline #15071.

Cerise

Cerise is one of several rose etchings produced in Crystal, and usually appears on stemline #15071. This etching is also found on stemline #15072.

Charmian

The Charmian etching was introduced in 1924 and discontinued in 1935. This iris motif was produced in Crystal with and without gold inlay and in Amber with gold inlay on stemline #14196.

Classic

One of the most popular patterns produced, Classic has remained a favorite pattern since its introduction in 1913. This figural motif etching was available in Crystal on stemlines #14185 and #15047; Crystal with Green trim on stemlines #15011 and #15016; and Rose Pink with Crystal trim on stemline #15024.

Coronet

The Coronet etching was produced in 1936 in Crystal on stemline #2822 and #17434. This etching was previously known as Avalon, c. 1933. Both patterns were produced at the Glassport, Pennsylvania, factory.

Deerwood

This popular etching of a forest scene was produced in Crystal on stemline #14196 at Factory R, and at the Glassport, Pennsylvania, factory in Rose Pink and Reflex Green on stemline #2809. Accessory pieces were available in Black with gold inlay.

Diana

The Diana etching was introduced on stemline #14196 in Crystal or Rose Pink in 1924. This stemline was decorated with the gold Apollo band in 1931. In 1932 this etching was available in Crystal or Mandarin on stemline #15042 with a gold or platinum Athens band. The etching has also been found on stemline #15042 in Crystal with a Minton platinum band. Diana was offered by the Montgomery Ward Co. in the Fall/Winter 1931-1932 catalog under their name, Empress Josephine. It was offered on stemline #15042 in Crystal or Mandarin Gold with platinum or gold bands in six items. The Mandarin goblet with Athens gold band was priced at $1.00 and a 7 1/2" salad plate at $1.59.

Eldorado

Produced in Crystal on stemline #14194, this bird motif etching was discontinued in 1929.

Elinor

This basket motif etching was introduced in 1924 on stemline #14194 and was available in Crystal or Green.

Empire

One of four Tiffin bird motif etchings, Empire was available in Rose Pink on stemlines #15018 and #15024 and in Crystal on stemline #15070.

Flanders

Flanders, one of the most collectible Tiffin floral patterns, was introduced in Crystal, and Rose Pink with Crystal trim in 1927 on stemline #15024. Mandarin with Crystal trim was available on this stemline in 1928, along with all Rose Pink, and Rose Pink with Green trim. Other stemlines available with the Flanders etching were the #15047 in Crystal or Mandarin, and the #15071 in Crystal.

Florence

The Florence etching was produced in Crystal on stemline #17328. This etching was known earlier as Cordelia, and was available on stemlines #15067 and #15072.

Fontaine

Fontaine, a French word meaning fountain, is another Tiffin bird motif etching which was produced in the late 1920s. It was discontinued in 1931. Very popular with collectors today in the Twilite color, Fontaine is also available in Crystal with Green trim, Twilite with Crystal trim, and Rose Pink, on stemline #15033. Fontaine is the only etching that was produced on the Twilite color.

Floris

The Floris etching was produced on the #15038 stemline in Crystal, Crystal with Green trim, and Rose Pink. This pattern is seldom seen today.

Fuchsia

The Fuchsia etching was introduced in 1935 in Crystal on the #15083 stemline. This etching was also offered as Silver Fuchsia in a 1938 price listing. A popular pattern with collectors today, Fuchsia was available on several post-1940 stems, including #17449, #17453, #17454 and #17687. The Fuchsia etching which appears on stemline #17457 is known as Blue Bonnet.

Hawe

A short-lived pattern, Hawe was discontinued in 1934. The etching was available on stemline #15072 in Crystal or Mandarin with Crystal trim.

Helena

The Helena etching was very popular on the #14188 stemline and was available in Rose Pink, Crystal, Amber or Green. It can also be found in Mandarin with Crystal trim on stemline #15066.

Isabella

The Isabella etching, which features a clipper ship motif, was produced in Crystal on stemline #14187.

Jap Lily

An early 1920's etching, Jap Lily is found on stemline #14179 in Crystal.

Julia

Produced in Crystal with Amber trim on stemline #15011, the Julia pattern was discontinued in 1935. The plates were offered in Crystal or Amber. The Julia etching was later produced on stemline #15001 in Crystal.

Juno

One of the few Tiffinware etchings available in the Topaz color, Juno was produced at Factory GES, (Glassport Etching Shop), Glassport, Pennsylvania, c. late 1920s. Other colors with the Juno etching are Reflex Green, Rose Pink and Crystal.

Lace

Lace is an all-over etching that was produced in a limited number of items. Footed #14185 table tumblers and ice teas were available; however, no stems were offered in this pattern. Colors available were Crystal with Amber, Blue or Green trim.

La Fleure

La Fleure, a French term meaning "the flower," features a lily-of-the-valley motif. Stemlines available were the #15024 which was available in Crystal, Rose Pink with Crystal trim, Rose Pink, and Mandarin with Crystal trim; #15022 in Mandarin with Crystal trim; and #15069 in Crystal in 1935. La Fleure was later reintroduced in Crystal as Blue Bell on the #15024 stemline.

La Salle

Available from 1932-1935, Lasalle was available in Crystal or Crystal with Mandarin trim on the #15070 stemline.

Luciana

A figural motif etching, Luciana was available on three stemlines: #15037 in Crystal with Black trim; #15043 in Crystal with Black trim; and #15016 in Crystal with Green trim. The shape for the #15016 stemline was designed by Virgil Loomis. Plates with the Luciana etching were available in Green or Black. This pattern was discontinued in 1931.

Melrose

Melrose was a popular etching which was produced intermittently from the mid 1920s through the 1970s. Early stemlines were: #13633 in Crystal, discontinued in 1935; #15018 in Crystal with Green trim, including Green plates; and #17356 in Crystal. Amber was available on an undetermined stemline. Later offerings included the #17358 and #17453 in Crystal, and #15074 and #17394 in Killarney. All stemlines were decorated with a Melrose band, which was sometimes gold encrusted.

Modernistic

Modernistic, an Art Deco etching was available in Green or Rose Pink on the #14185 stemline.

Navarre

The Navarre pattern was introduced in 1932 in Crystal or Mandarin with Crystal trim on stemline #15068, and discontinued in 1934.

Nymph

This figural motif etching was produced in the late 1920s in Crystal with Green trim on stemline #15011.

Oneida

Oneida was produced in the early 1930s on stemline #348 in Crystal with Blue, Green or Red enameled etching at Factory GES (Glassport Etching Shop). This line was also available with a platinum band. The Oneida etching was renamed Hostess in 1936 and was offered on the #2823 stemline in Crystal.

Persian Pheasant

An early 1930s bird motif etching, Persian Pheasant was offered in Crystal, Rose Pink, and Crystal with Green trim on stemline #15037. Plates and centerpiece bowls were available in Green. Stemline #15037 was discontinued in 1935. Other stemlines with the Persian Pheasant etching were the #17358 and #17392, which were produced in Crystal.

Poppy

The Poppy etching was introduced in Crystal in 1924 on stemline #14196.

Princess

Princess, a poppy motif etching was available in Crystal on stemline #13643 from its introduction in 1913 until discontinued in 1935.

Psyche

Psyche was introduced in 1926 in Crystal with Green trim on stemline #15016. This figural motif etching was also produced on the #15003, #15011, and the #15039 stemlines in Crystal with Green trim. Psyche was also available in Crystal on the #15039 stemline which was discontinued in 1931.

Queen Astrid

A floral motif etching, Queen Astrid was produced in the late 1930s in Crystal on stemlines #17351 and #17358. Occasionally, this etching is found with gold inlay.

Rosalind

Introduced in 1930, the Rosalind etching was produced in Crystal, Mandarin, and Rose Pink on stemline #15042 and discontinued in 1935.

Rose Marie

One of several rose motif etchings produced at Factory R, Rose Marie was offered in Crystal on stemlines #15024 and #15071.

Roses

The Roses pattern was produced in Crystal on stemline #14180 and discontinued in 1931.

Special Thistle

Special Thistle was produced at Factory R in the mid-1920s on stemline #14197 in Crystal. This pattern, originally produced by the Central Glass Company, Wheeling West Virginia, as early as 1908, was listed by Central Glass as Scotch Thistle. Identical stemlines were used by both factories; tableware items can be identified by known factory shapes.

Thistle

Available from 1920 through 1934, Thistle was produced on stemline #14180 in Crystal. The Thistle etching differs from the Special Thistle pattern which has a long drooping leaf.

Tourainne

Tourainne, another rose motif etching was available in Crystal on stemline #17328.

Vintage

One of several grape motif patterns produced at Factory R, the Vintage etching was introduced in 1921 in Crystal or Green on stemline #14180. A full tableware line was offered in these two colors. Vintage was discontinued in 1931.

Wallpaper

An all-over etching, Wallpaper was produced in a limited number of items. No footed stemmed pieces were offered. Footed #14185 table tumblers, ice teas, jugs and 10" bud vases were available in Crystal with Amber, Blue, or Green trim. An Amber corset vase has also been seen with Wallpaper etching.

Adam

Above: Crystal #14178: Sundae, Hollow Stem Champagne, Saucer Champagne, Goblet, Wine, Oyster Cocktail. All Wide Optic. $15-25, $25-35, $15-25, $20-30, $20-30, $15-25

Above right: Crystal #14178, 10 oz. Goblet, Wide Optic. $20-30

Right: Crystal: #14251, Low Grape Fruit with #881 liner and silver ring; #102, 2 qt. Jug. Both Wide Optic. $35-45, $175-225

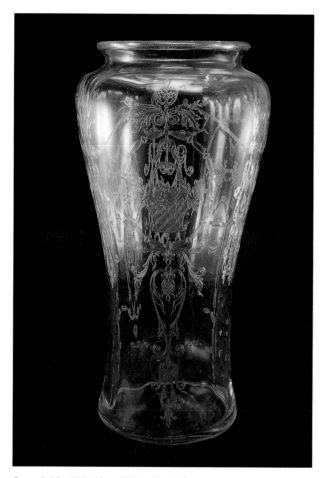

Crystal #6, 13" h. Vase, Wide Optic. $125-175

Amber #33, 10" h. Vase. $100-125

Detail of Adam etching.

21

Arcadian

Crystal with Green trim #9712, 2 qt. Jug, Wide Optic.
$225-275

Detail of Arcadian etching.

Rose Pink with Crystal trim #15024, Saucer Champagne,
Wide Optic. $20-30

Aster

Crystal: #114, 3 pt. Jug; #13628, 9 oz. Goblet. Both Wide Optic. $175-225, $15-25

Berian

The Berian etching illustrated on this United States Glass Company catalog page dated April 30, 1934 includes an unusual handled decanter. Also note the footed Whiskey and hollow stem Champagne.

15074. 13 oz. Goblet, Optic

15074. 8 oz. Saucer Champagne Optic

15074. 8 oz. Sundae, Optic

15074. 6 oz. Cafe Parfait Optic

15074. 4½ oz. Claret, Optic

15074. 3 oz. Wine, Optic

15074. 4 oz. Cocktail, Optic

15074. 1¼ oz. Cordial, Optic

15074. 12½ oz. Iced Tea, Footed Optic

15074. 9½ oz. Table, Footed Optic

15074. 4½ oz. Seltzer, Footed Optic

15074. 2¾ oz. Whiskey, Footed Optic

14196. 4½ oz. Oyster Cocktail Optic

13771. 5 oz. H/S Champagne Cut Stem, Optic

5831. 7½" Plate
5831. 6" Plate

5831. Sugar

5831. Cream

5831. 6" Tall Comport

5831. Single Candleholder

5831. 11¼" Centerpiece Bowl

5831. 2-Light Candelabrum

1070. 12 oz. Finger Bowl Optic

14185. 32 oz. Ftd. Hld. Decanter & Stopper, Optic

5831. 10¾" Cake Plate, Hld.

14194. 54 oz. Ftd. Jug & Cover, Optic

Bridal

15073. 9 oz.
Goblet, Optic

15073. 5½ oz.
Saucer Champagne
Optic

15073. 5½ oz.
Sundae, Optic

15073. 5½ oz.
Café Parfait
Optic

15073. 5½ oz.
Champagne, Optic

15073. 4 oz.
Claret, Optic

15073. 2½ oz.
Wine, Optic

15073. 2 oz.
Sherry, Optic

15073. 3 oz.
Cocktail, Optic

15073. 1 oz.
Cordial, Optic

15073. 1 oz.
Pousse Café
Optic

15073. 2¼ oz.
Whiskey, Ftd., Optic

15073. 4½ oz.
Seltzer, Ftd., Optic

15073. 9½ oz.
Table, Ftd., Optic

15073. 12½ oz.
Iced Tea, Ftd., Optic

14196. 4½ oz.
Oyster Cocktail, Optic

A June 28, 1934 United States Glass Company catalog page illustrating a number of assorted items in the Bridal plate etching. Note the unusual platinum encrusted band.

TIFFIN

24

1070. 12 oz.
Finger Bowl
Optic

5831. 6¾ oz.
Sugar

5831. 5¼ oz.
Cream

5831. Single
Candleholder

5831. 11¼" Centerpiece Bowl

5831. 2 Light
Candelabrum

8833. 8" Plate
8814. 6" Plate

5831. 6" Tall
Comport

5831. 10¼" Cake Plate, Hld.

14185. 32 oz. Decanter & Stopper, Optic

128. 66 oz. Jug, Optic

1930 United States Glass
Company catalog page
illustrating Bridal plate
etching.

Byzantine

FACTORY "R" TIFFIN, OHIO
United States Glass Company, Pittsburgh, Pa., U. S. A.
PLATE ETCHED "BYZANTINE" DESIGN
Furnished in (Wide Optic)
All Crystal, Crystal-Black Trim and Mandarin-Crystal Trim
Note:—For complete itemization of this line, see other side

106-1-27-31

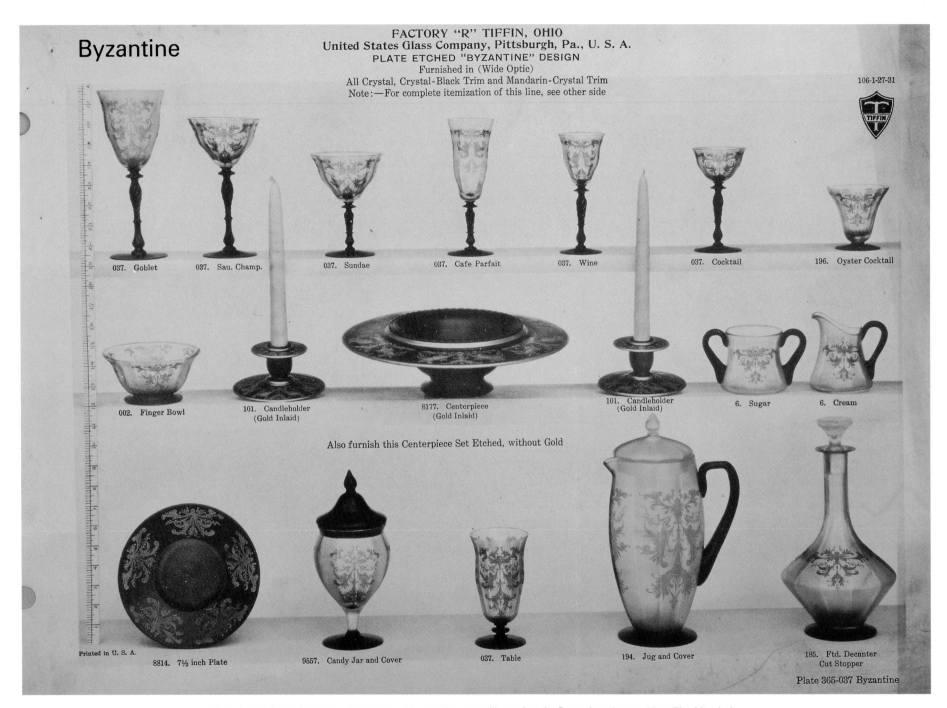

037. Goblet   037. Sau. Champ.   037. Sundae   037. Cafe Parfait   037. Wine   037. Cocktail   196. Oyster Cocktail

002. Finger Bowl   101. Candleholder (Gold Inlaid)   8177. Centerpiece (Gold Inlaid)   101. Candleholder (Gold Inlaid)   6. Sugar   6. Cream

Also furnish this Centerpiece Set Etched, without Gold

8814. 7½ inch Plate   9557. Candy Jar and Cover   037. Table   194. Jug and Cover   185. Ftd. Decanter Cut Stopper

Printed in U. S. A.

Plate 365-037 Byzantine

United States Glass Company January 1, 1931, catalog page illustrating the Byzantine plate etching. The Mandarin with Black trim color combination is considered extremely scarce.

GIFT ITEMS INNUMERABLE

*F*ROM the most delicately blown Tiffinware to pressed wares in popular colors, the UNITED STATES line offers a great number of items most suitable for gift purposes. Not only for June, but for every other time of the year, a showing of gift items from our lines will help build up sales and good will.

The Bath Salt Jar with cover is ordered in quantities of 600 by one leading store. Available in black and colors and especially attractive in black with lustre finish.

Remember—"United States Glass Wares Give Complete Service."

No. 16256—Bath Salt with cover. Made in black, black satin, green and pink. Useful as a vase without cover. Can be had that way, too.

No. R9557 Candy Jar and Cover. Crystal with foot and cover in black. It is beautiful Tiffinware at its best. Decorated with the popular "Byzantine" etching. Stemware to match also attractive.

Here are two items from the 310½ Tableware line in the popular "Rosemary" etching. They are a footed mint wafer and a footed marmalade. Made in both pink and green. The line includes many other attractive items.

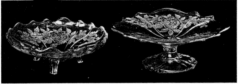

UNITED STATES GLASS CO.

PITTSBURGH

Sales Offices in all Principal Cities

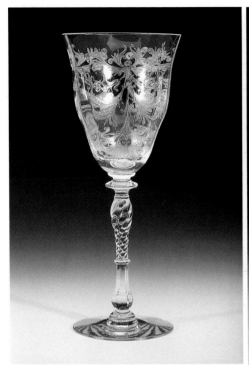

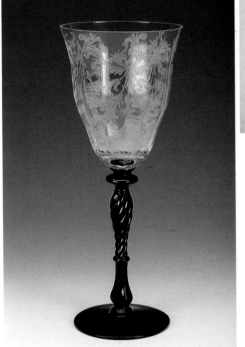

Top left: Crystal #15037, Goblet, Wide Optic. $25-35

Bottom left: Crystal with Black trim #15037, Goblet, Wide Optic. $45-55

Above: Crystal with Black trim: #15037, Sundae, Café Parfait, Goblet, Cocktail, Saucer Champagne, Ice Tea; #6, Cream and Sugar. All Wide Optic. $35-45, $45-55, $45-55, $35-45, $40-50, $35-45, $100-125 set

Above: Detail of Byzantine etching.

Top right: Black: #101, 5" Low Candleholders, center candleholder with gold inlay; #8177, 12" Centerpiece Bowl. $45-65 each, $65-85 with gold, $75-100

Bottom right: Crystal #15048, Goblet, Wide Optic, platinum Leaf band. $35-45

Cadena

Crystal #15065, Goblet, Wide Optic. $25-35

Above: Crystal: #15065, Saucer Champagne; #14194, Jug with cover; #15065, Cordial. All Wide Optic. $20-30, $225-275, $50-60

Top right: Detail of Cadena etching.

Bottom right: Crystal #2642, 6 1/4" Rose Jar, Wide Optic. $75-100

Mandarin #14185, 32 oz. Decanter, Wide Optic, faceted Crystal stopper. $250-300

Capri

Crystal #15071, Goblet, Wide Optic. $20-30

Mandarin with Crystal trim #15065, Goblet, Sundae, Cocktail. All Wide Optic. $35-45, 30-40, 30-40

Detail of Capri etching.

Cerise

Crystal: #5831, 5" Mayonnaise, with 7" plate, Wide Optic; #5831, 12 1/2" Handled Cake Plate; #15071, Cordial, Wide Optic; #9743, Table Bell, Wide Optic; #15071, Goblet, Wide Optic. $35-45 set, $25-35, $35-45, $30-40, $15-25

Top right: Crystal #15071, Cordial, Wide Optic. $30-40

Bottom right: Detail of Cerise etching.

32

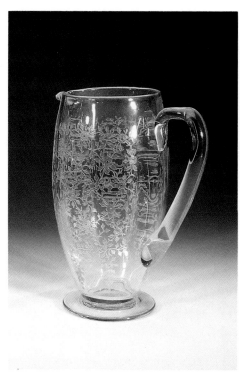

Crystal #14194, 2 qt. Jug, Wide Optic.
$175-225

Crystal #15360, 7" 2-Lite Candelabrum; #2, Salt
and Pepper, Wide Optic. $35-45, $35-45 set.

Charmian

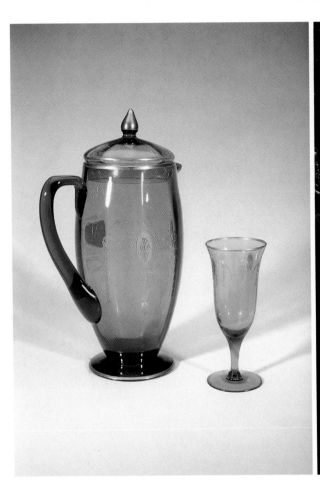

Amber #14194, 2 qt. Jug with cover; #14180, Café Parfait.
Both with Wide Optic and gold inlay. $400-500, $35-45

Detail of gold inlay.

A March 31, 1924, *China, Glass and Lamps* advertisement
illustrating the #14199 goblet with the #281 Needle etching, the
#14196 goblet with the Diana plate etching, the #14199 goblet
with wire optic, the #14196 goblet with the Charmian plate
etching, and the #14199 goblet with the cut #40 design.

No. 196. Goblet.

No. 196. Sau Champ

No. 196. Sundae.

No. 180. Parfait.

No. 196. Claret.

No. 196. Wine.

No. 196. Cocktail.

No. 630. Oyster Cocktail.

No. 196/8814-6 in. Finger Bowl and Plate.

No. 8833-8 in. Salad Plate.

No. 354-5 oz.

No. 354. Table. Also furnish No. 354-12 oz. Ice Tea.

No. 194-2 Qt. Ftd. Jug and Cover. Also furnish without Cover.

Plate 365-Charmian Gold Inlaid.

Catalog page featuring the Charmian etching with gold inlay c. 1924.

35

Classic

Above: Crystal #354, Handled Tumbler; #14185, Goblet, Sundae; #354, Table Tumbler; #14185, Saucer Champagne, Seltzer, Ice Tea, Whiskey, Wine, Cordial; #13882, 22 oz. Grape Fruit and Liner; #14185, Café Parfait. $55-65, $25-35, $20-30, $35-45, $20-30, $20-30, $20-30, $40-50, $30-40, $65-85, $75-95, $50-60

Top left: Crystal #14185, Goblet. $25-35

Bottom left: Detail of Classic etching.

Opposite page; top left: Crystal: #14185, 6" Low Comport, Wide Optic; #14179, 30 oz. Decanter, Wide Optic; #151, 6 1/2" Whipped Cream Set. $65-85, $275-325, $75-100 set

Top right: Crystal: #115, 2 qt. Jug; #6 Cream; #114, 2 qt. Tall Jug. All Wide Optic. $250-300, $65-85, $300-350

Bottom left: Crystal: #8833, 8" Plate; #8818, 10" Plate; #8814, 6" Plate; #23, 8" Vase, Wide Optic. $20-30, $100-125, $15-25, $175-225

Bottom right: Crystal #5831, 6 1/2" Tall Comport; #5831, 11" Centerpiece; #14185, 10 1/4" h. Bud Vase, 6" Bud Vase. $75-100, $150-175, $45-65, $35-55

36

Rose Pink with Crystal trim #15024, Saucer Champagne, Goblet, Wine; #14185, Seltzer. All Wide Optic. $55-75, $65-85, $65-85, $45-55

Rose Pink with Crystal trim #15024, Goblet, Wide Optic. $65-85

Crystal with Reflex Green trim: #14185, Seltzer; #15011, Goblet; Crystal with Nile Green trim #15016, Cordial. All Wide Optic. $45-55, $65-85, $125-150

Top left: Crystal with Nile Green trim #9758, 5" Candleholders. $175-225 pair

Bottom left: Crystal with Nile Green trim #15011, Goblet, Wide Optic. $65-85

Crystal with Nile Green trim: #6, Sugar and Cream; #9557, ½ lb. Candy Jar with cover. All Wide Optic. $150-200 set, $125-175

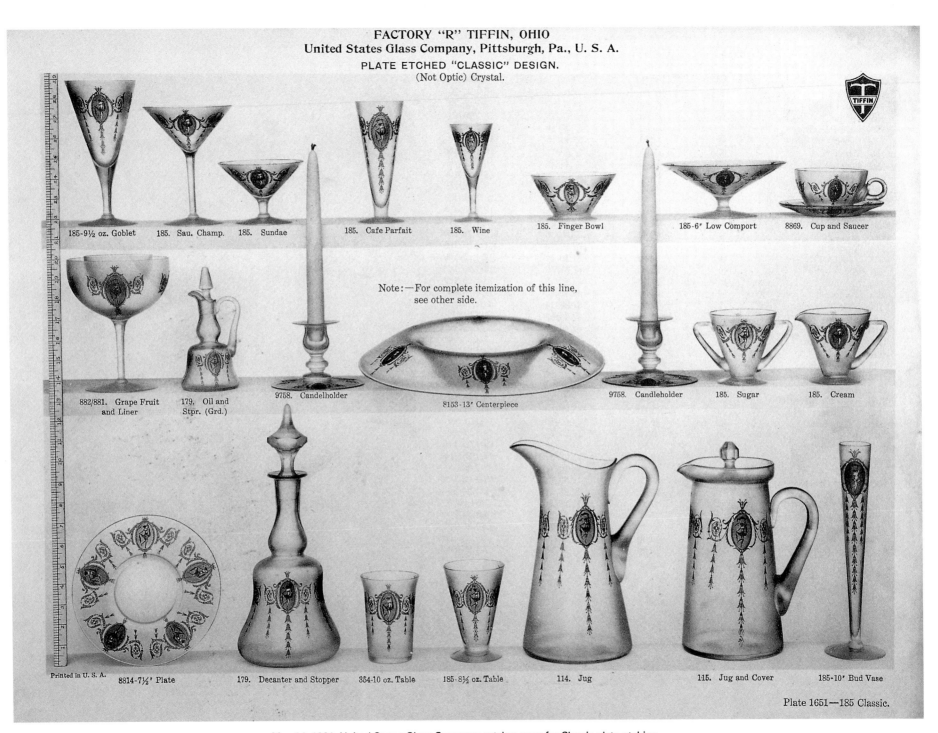

Note:—For complete itemization of this line, see other side.

185-9½ oz. Goblet 185. Sau. Champ. 185. Sundae 185. Cafe Parfait 185. Wine 185. Finger Bowl 185-6″ Low Comport 8869. Cup and Saucer

882/881. Grape Fruit and Liner 179. Oil and Stpr. (Grd.) 9758. Candelholder 8153-13″ Centerpiece 9758. Candleholder 185. Sugar 185. Cream

Printed in U. S. A.

8814-7½″ Plate 179. Decanter and Stopper 354-10 oz. Table 185-8½ oz. Table 114. Jug 115. Jug and Cover 185-10″ Bud Vase

Plate 1651—185 Classic.

May 14, 1931, United States Glass Company catalog page for Classic plate etching.

40

		Cap. oz.	Price	Carton	$1.25 Barrel				Cap. oz.	Price	Carton	$1.25 Barrel
185	Goblet,	9½	$15.00	3/.50/25	6/70		8869	Cup.	8	$18.75	1/.25/9	15/100
185	Sau. Champ.,	6½	15.00	3/.75/27	5/70		8869	Saucer,		20.85	1/.10/7	30/155
185	Sundae,	5	15.00	3/.75/25	8/75		8869	Cup and Saucer Set,		39.60	1/.35/16	10/120
185	Cafe Parfait,	6	15.00	3/.35/16	12/95		185	Ftd. Sugar,	7	40.80	1/.25/11	8/80
185	Claret,	5	14.55	3/.40/18	12/90		185	Ftd. Cream,	6½	37.20	1/.25/11	8/80
185	Wine,	2½	14.35	3/.30/12	20/100		185	Ftd. S. and C. Set,		78.00	1/.35/21	4/80
185	Cocktail,	3¼	14.35	3/.45/18	10/75		185	(6") Ftd. Bud Vase,		14.40	3/.30/14	18/100
185	Cordial,	1	14.10	3/.20/7	56/100		185	(10") Ftd. Bud Vase,		15.90	3/.50/25	7/80
185	Ftd. Finger Bowl,	8	19.00	3/.30/23	8/85		5831	(2 Hdl.) Bon Bon,		22.95	3/.55/30	6/80
8814	(6") Plate,		19.50	3/.30/24	20/135		5831	Candleholder,		21.45	1/.35/15	7/85
8814	(7½") Plate,		24.00	3/.30/27	12/120		5831	Centerpiece,		73.80	½/.60/28	1¾/90
8833	(8") Plate,		28.50	3/.30/27	8/117		5831	Celery Tray,		30.75	3/.60/37	
8818	(10") Plate,		40.50	3/.60/65	6½/140		5831	Ftd. Comport (Small),		22.50	3/.45/22	8/75
354	Tumbler,	5	9.90	3/.30/12	31/105		5831	Creme Soup,		23.10	3/.55/20	6/75
354	Table,	10	10.40	3/.40/17	17/100		5831	Creme Soup and Plate,		46.65	1/.40/18	4/85
354	Ale,	10	10.40	3/.35/16	16/105		5831	Cup,		15.45	3/.40/18	12/95
354	Ice Tea,	12	11.10	3/.40/18	13/102		5831	Saucer,		19.50	3/.30/28	20/125
354	Ice Tea,	14	12.30	3/.40/20	11/95		5831	Cup and Saucer Set,		34.95	1½/.45/22	8/110
185	Ftd. Whiskey,	2¼	12.90	3/.30/14	30/105		5831	Mayonnaise Bowl,		24.00	3/.45/24	8/95
185	Ftd. Seltzer,	5	13.30	3/.40/13	16/95		5831	Mayonnaise Plate,		23.55	3/.30/25	14/130
185	Ftd. Table,	8½	13.70	3/.45/17	12/90		5831	Mayonnaise Ladle,		4.65	—	
185	Ftd. Ice Tea,	12	14.70	3/.45/19	9/80		5831	Mayonnaise Set,		52.15	1/.30/18	4½/95
114	(2 Qt.) Jug,	66	75.00	1/.85/61	1¼/90		5831	Nappy (2 Hdl.),		22.95	3/.50/20	8/80
115	Jug and Cover,	62	80.00	1/.65/49	1⅔/90		5831	Pickle Tray,		24.60	3/.45/25	7/85
9758	Candleholder,		29.10	1/.40/14	6/85		5831	2 Hdl. Plate, (Small)		22.95	3/.30/24	15/130
8153	Centerpiece,		103.00	¾/.75/42	1⅓/90		5831	(6") Plate,		19.80	3/.30/28	20/125
185	(6") Low Comport,		45.00	1/.45/21	4/75		5831	(7½") Plate,		24.15	3/.30/28	10/130
179	Qt. Dectr. and C/S.,	30	91.50	½/.30/20	2½/95		5831	(9½") Plate,		37.20	3/.50/40	7/130
882	Grape Fruit,	22	40.80	1/.45/16	2½/60		5831	Platter,		78.00	½/.25/12	4/115
881	Ftd. Liner,	6	6.00	1/.15/7	18/90		5831	Sugar,		28.80	1/.30/10	8/90
185	Ftd. Ind. Salt,	¾	12.90	3/.30/7	60/115		5831	Cream,		28.80	1/.30/10	8/90
179	Oil and stpr. Grd.,	3¾	48.25	3/.45/18	12/125		5831	Sugar and Cream Set,		57.60	1/.45/20	4½/95

A May 14, 1931, United States Glass Company price listing for the Classic plate etching.

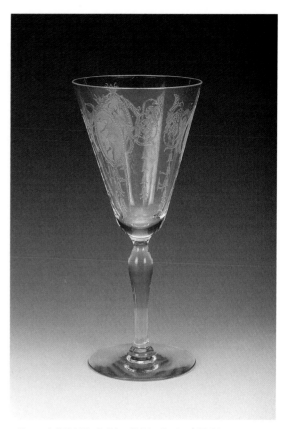

Crystal #15047, Goblet, Wide Optic. $20-30

Coronet

Top left: Crystal #17434, Saucer Champagne. $15-25

Top right: Detail of Coronet etching.

Bottom left: Crystal #319, 10 1/2" h. 2-handled Vase. $65-85

Bottom right: Crystal: #2642, 6" Rose Jar, Wide Optic; #15360, 10 1/2" Centerpiece; #15360, 3-Lite Candelabra. The candelabra was also listed as #8220 in an earlier United States Glass Company catalog. $45-65, $45-65, $100-125 pair

Deerwood

Top center: Rose Pink, Reflex Green #151, 7" Sweet Pea Vases; Reflex Green #330, 7 3/4" h. Conic Candy Jar and cover. $120-145 each, $125-175

Center: Reflex Green: #15151, 12" Celery Tray; #9395, Cup and Saucer; #330, 6 1/4" Whipped Cream and Ladle. $65-85, $75-100, $100-125

Bottom center: Reflex Green: #8177, 12" Centerpiece Bowl; #101, 5" Low Candleholder. $100-125, $65-85

Top right: Crystal #14196, Goblet, Wide Optic. $40-50

Bottom right: Detail of Deerwood etching.

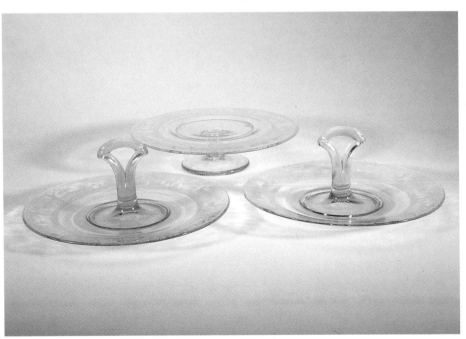

Top left: Crystal with Pink or Green trim: Goblet, Wine, Saucer Champagne, with optic. This stemline has not been identified as a United States Glass Company product. $45-55, $45-55, $40-50

Top right: Rose Pink #330, 10" Cheese and Cracker set. $100-125 set

Bottom left: Rose Pink #330, 10" Low Foot Salver; Pink, Green 10" Handled Cake Plates with Deerwood etching on a Paden City Glass Company blank. $125-150, $45-65 each

Bottom right: Rose Pink: #2809, Goblet; #14196, Goblet, Medium Optic. $45-55 each

Black: #179, Cream and Sugar; #8177, 7" h. Compote, gold inlay. $150-200 set, $175-225

45

Top: Detail of Deerwood etching.

Bottom: Black #330, 10" Cheese and Cracker set, gold inlay. $175-225 set

Top: Black: #336, 10" 2-handled Cake Plate; #8177, 10" Celery Tray, gold inlay. $150-200 each

Bottom: Black: #101, 5" Candleholders; #8177, 12" Centerpiece, gold inlay. $150-200 pair, $150-200

46

UNITED STATES GLASS COMPANY, PITTSBURGH, PA., U. S. A.
ETCHED "DEERWOOD" DESIGN.
Furnished on Green or Pink Glass.
The Prices given are per Dozen, List.

Factory "GES"
150-12-2-29

No. 2809
Goblet
$10.00

No. 2809
Sau. Champ.
$10.00

No. 2809
Wine
$9.50

No. 2809
Cocktail
$9.50

No. 2808-Footed
Ice Tea Tumbler
$10.00

No. 2808-Footed
Table Tumbler
$10.00

No. 9395-Cup and Saucer
$19.00

No. 8133-Breakfast Dish
$16.00

No. 151-Celery Tray
$22.20

Note; For other items listed in this Design, See Plate No. 354

No. 8859-10″ Dinner Plate
$23.75

No. 8836-7½″ Salad Plate
$11.80

No. 8836-5½″ Plate
$10.60

No. 6471-10″ Vase
$23.75

Printed in U. S. A.

Plate No. 353

December 2, 1929, United States Glass Company catalog page featuring the Deerwood plate etching. Note that this ware was produced at Factory GES (Glassport Etching Shop), Glassport, Pennsylvania, and marketed as Tiffinware.

UNITED STATES GLASS COMPANY, PITTSBURGH, PA., U. S. A.
ETCHED "DEERWOOD" DESIGN.
Furnished on Green or Pink Glass.
12-Piece Assortment Illustrated.

Factory "GES"
150-12-2-29

No. 330-102 Low Foot
Comport Flared
$23.75

No. 151-7" Sweet Pea Vase
Rolled Edge
$16.00

The Prices given are per Dozen, List.

No. 8105 10" Salad
Straight Edge
$22.20

No. 330-Whipped Cream
and Ladle
$18.00

No. 101-Low
Candleholder
$12.75

No. 8177-12" Centerpiece
$28.50

Note; For other items listed in this Design, See Plate No. 353

No. 101-Low
Candleholder
$12.75

No. 330-Conic
Candy Jar and Cover
$19.00

No. 179-Sugar
$11.10

No. 329-6" Candy Box and Cover
$19.00

No. 179-Cream
$11.10

No. 179-Sugar and Cream Set $22.20

No. 330-10" Handled Cake Plate
$23.75

No. 330-10" Low Foot Salver
$23.75

No. 330-Cheese and Cracker Set
$30.00

Printed in U.S.A.

Plate No. 354

December 2, 1929, United States Glass Company catalog page featuring the Deerwood plate etching. Note the Factory GES designation.

Diana

FACTORY "R" TIFFIN, OHIO
United States Glass Company, Pittsburgh, Pa., U. S. A.
(Wide Optic)
PLATINUM ENC. "ATHENS-DIANA," Crystal, or
GOLD ENC. "ATHENS-DIANA," Mandarin.

042. Goblet
Mandarin-Gold
Encrusted

042. Sau. Champ.
Platinum Encrusted

042. Sundae

042. Parfait

042. Cocktail

196. Oyster Cocktail

Note:-For complete itemization of this line, see other side.

041. Finger Bowl

8820-7½" Plate

042. Table

128. Jug

251. Grape Fruit
and Liner

Plate 765-042 Athens-Diana

Printed in U. S. A.

United States Glass Company catalog page illustrating the Diana plate etching and the Athens gold band c. 1932.

Top left: A January 25, 1926, *China, Glass and Lamps* advertisement featuring the Diana plate etching and the Apollo gold band.

Bottom left: Crystal: #15042, Goblet, Cordial; #8820, 7 1'2" Plate; #5831, 6" Handled Nappy; #15042 Saucer Champagne. All Wide Optic and platinum Athens band. $40-50, $55-75, $20-30, $35-45, $35-45

Top right: Crystal #15042, Goblet, Wide Optic, platinum Athens band. $40-50

Bottom right: Detail of Diana etching.

Eldorado

Detail of Eldorado etching.

Crystal #14194, 9 oz. Goblet, 9 oz. Table Tumbler, 12 oz. Handled Tumbler. All Wide Optic. $20-30, $15-25, $25-35

Crystal: #14194, 2 qt. Jug and cover; # 14194, 1 qt. Covered Tankard. Both Wide Optic. The tankard is rare in any pattern. $225-275, $275-325

Crystal #14194, 9 oz. Goblet, Wide Optic. $20-30

Elinor

Crystal #14194, 9 oz. Goblet, Wide Optic, gold band. $25-35

Detail of Elinor etching.

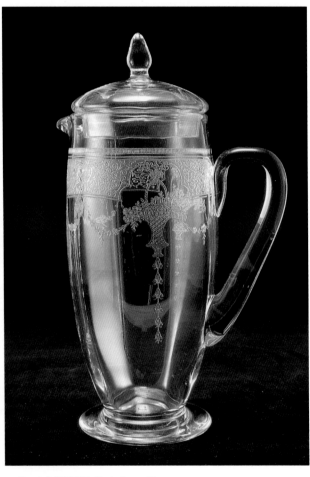

Crystal #14194, 2 qt. Jug with cover, Wide Optic. $225-275

Left: Rose Pink #15018, Goblet, Table Tumbler; #14194, 2 qt. Jug with cover. All Wide Optic. $65-85, $45-55, $350-400

Right: May, 1928, "Good Housekeeping" magazine advertisement featuring the Empire plate etching.

Flanders

Crystal: #15024, Cordial, Café Parfait, Sundae; #8869, Cup; #15024, Wine; #14251, 20 oz. Grape Fruit with #881 Liner; #15024, Goblet, Saucer Champagne, Cocktail; #5831, Cup; #020 Ice Tea; #196 Oyster Cocktail; #020 Table Tumbler, Whiskey, Seltzer. All stems Wide Optic. $65-85, $40-50, $25-35, $55-75, $30-40, $75-100, $30-40, $25-35, $25-35, $45-65, $30-40, $25-35, $25-35, $50-60, $25-35

Crystal: #6 Sugar and Cream, Wide Optic; 9" 2-Lite Candelabrum, unknown line number; #14185, 4 1/2" Finger Bowl, Wide Optic; #5831, 7" 2-Lite Candelabrum; #14185 10", 8" h. Bud Vases; #5831 Sugar and Cream. $100-150, $65-85, $35-45, $55-75, $50-60. $40-50, $65-85 set

Crystal #15024, Goblet, Wide Optic. $30-40

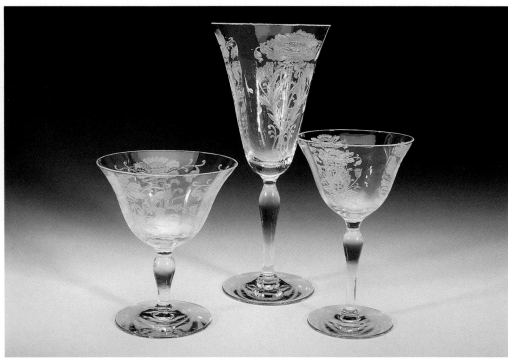

Crystal #15047, Sundae, Goblet, Cocktail, Wide Optic. $20-30, $25-35, $20-30

Detail of Flanders etching.

Crystal: #9758, 5" Low Candlesticks; #5831, 12" Centerpiece Bowl. $125-175 pair, $100-125

Top left: Crystal #9557, ½ lb. Candy Jar and cover, Wide Optic. $150-200

Top right: Crystal: 12"h. Chinese Hurricane Shades, unknown line number; #8153, 13" Centerpiece. $450-500 pair, $125-150

Bottom left: Crystal: #15310, 11 1/4" Footed Centerpiece Bowl; #5831, 6 1/2" Tall Comport; #5831, 10 1/2" Celery Tray. $55-75, $75-100, $45-65

Bottom right: Crystal: #5831, 6 1/4" Handled Bon Bon; #5831, 9 1/2" Nouvelle Bowl; #5831, 6 1/4" Handled Bowl; #8897, 12 1/4" 5-Part Relish Tray. $35-45, $55-75, $35-45, $75-100

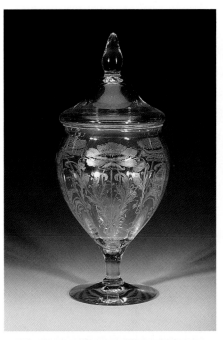

Above: Rose Pink with Crystal trim: #020, Table Tumbler; #15024, Goblet, Sundae, Saucer Champagne, Cordial; #2, Almond Cup. All Wide Optic. $40-50, $50-60, $45-55, $45-55, $100-125, $50-75

Top right: Rose Pink #004, 6" h. blown Compote, Wide Optic. $250-300

Bottom right: Rose Pink #179, 7 3/4" h. Conic Candy Jar and cover. $225-275

Bottom center: Rose Pink #9758, 5" Low Candlesticks; #5831, 12" Centerpiece Bowl. $250-300 pair, $200-250

Rose Pink with Reflex
Green trim #15024, Goblet,
Sundae, Saucer Cham-
pagne. All Wide Optic. $75-
100, $65-90, $65-90

Mandarin #15047, Cordial,
Wide Optic. $75-100

Crystal #15071, Saucer
Champagne, Wide Optic.
$20-30

Mandarin with Crystal trim
#15024, Saucer Champagne,
Wine; #020 Table Tumbler.
All Wide Optic. $25-35, $30-
40, $25-35

Rose Pink, Mandarin, Crystal #14194, 2 qt. Jugs with Covers, Wide Optic. $475-550, $325-375, $300-350

No.	Item	Cap. in oz.	Rose Cry. Tr.	All Crystal	Doz. to Bbl.	Wgt. of Bbl.
	Price List					
024	Goblet	9	$13.80	$13.05	5	70
024	Sau. Champ.	6	13.80	13.05	5	70
024	Sundae	6	13.30	12.60	8	75
024	Cafe Parfait	4½	13.80	13.05	10	80
024	Claret	5	13.30	12.60	11	80
024	Wine	3	12.80	12.30	13	80
024	Cocktail	3½	12.80	12.30	10	80
024	Cordial	1½	12.30	12.00	22	80
630	Oyster Cocktail	4	13.30	12.60	19	80
185	Finger Bowl, Ftd.	8	21.90	18.90	8	85
8814	Plate (Not Optic) 6″		15.00	14.25	20	135
8833	Plate (Not Optic) 8″		23.25	21.75	8	117
8818	Plate (Not Optic) 10″		30.00	28.50	6½	140
020	Tumbler, Ftd. Whiskey	2	13.00	10.20	40	105
020	Tumbler, Ftd. Seltzer	5	13.30	10.60	18	90
020	Tumbler, Ftd. Table	10	13.80	11.00	11	90
020	Tumbler, Ftd. Ice Tea	12	14.80	12.40	9	90
194	Ftd. Jug and Cover	54	85.00	71.50	1½	85
194	Ftd. Jug. only	54	73.00	62.00	1¾	85
194	Ftd. Jug Cover only .		12.00	9.50		
251	Grape Fruit	20	33.60	30.80	3½	65
881	Ftd. Liner (Crys. Not Opt. Not Dec.),	6	6.00	6.00	18	90
6	Sugar and Cream Set		57.00	51.00	5	120
6	Sugar	9	30.00	26.70	9	120
6	Cream	6½	27.00	24.30	12	120
179	Decanter, Cut Stopper	32		76.50	2½	95
624	Qt. Decanter and Stopper		90.00		1½	90
337	Hdld. Cake Plate (All Rose)		45.00		1¾	85
320	Hdld. Cake Plate			42.00		
9758	Low Candleholder (All Rose)		25.20	23.70	6	85
329	(6″) Candy Box (All Rose)		30.90	24.60	3¾	75
329	(6″) Candy Box and Cover (All Rose)		45.00	37.80	3½	75
179	Candy Jar (All Rose)		29.10	26.85	3½	90
179	Candy Jar and Cover (All Rose)		45.00	40.50	3	105
8153	(13″) Centerpiece (All Rose)		75.00	75.00	1⅓	90
337	Cheese and Cracker Set (All Rose)		66.00		3	135
151	Cheese and Cracker Set			55.20		
004	(6″) High Comport		57.00		2½	65
319	(7½″) High Comport (All Rose)		45.00	38.40	2	75
8869	Cup and Saucer Set		30.60	30.60	10	120
194	(4″) Deep Ftd. Nappy (All Rose)		15.90		15	110
194	(8″) Deep Ftd. Nappy (All Rose)		60.00		1½	75
8105	(10″) Salad Bowl (All Rose)		42.00	32.50	3½	125
179	(11″) Table Centre (All Rose)		45.00	40.50	2	100
2	(8″) Vase (All Rose)		18.00		5	85
151	(8″) Dahlia Vase (All Rose)		48.00	42.75	3	110
151	Whip Cream and Ladle (All Rose)		42.00	33.90	4	120

October 8, 1928, United States Glass Company price listing for Flanders plate etching.

Opposite page: October 8, 1928, United States Glass Company catalog page featuring Flanders plate etching.

FACTORY "R", TIFFIN, OHIO.
United States Glass Company, Pittsburgh, Pa., U. S. A.
ETCHED "FLANDERS" DESIGN.
Furnished (Wide Optic) Rose—Crystal Trim and All Crystal.

100-10-8-28

Note; For complete itemization of this line
see other side.

024—9 oz.
Goblet

024—6 oz.
Saucer Champ.

024. Sundae

024. Cafe Parf.

024—5 oz. Claret

024—3 oz. Wine

024—3½ oz.
Cocktail

630. Oyster
Cocktail

Printed in U. S. A.

8833—8 in. Salad Plate
(Not Optic)

185. Finger Bowl

020—12 oz.
Ice Tea

194—2 Qt. Jug and
Cover. Also furnish
without Cover

No. 6 Sugar

No. 6 Cream

Plate 365—Flanders

61

Florence

Top left: Crystal #15072, Ice Tea, Goblet, Cordial, Wide Optic. $20-30, $20-30, $40-50

Top center: Crystal #15072, 9 oz. Goblet, Wide Optic. $15-25

Bottom left: *China, Glass, and Lamps,* March 12, 1928.

Bottom center: Crystal with Green trim #032, 9 oz. Table Tumbler; #15033, Goblet; #4 Sugar and Cream; #14194, 8" Deep Footed Nappy. All Wide Optic. $30-40, $35-45, $125-175, $100-125

Bottom right: Crystal with Green trim #15033, Goblet, Wide Optic. $35-45

Fontaine

Interesting New United States Stemware

tall. This cutting is a departure from the type of cuttings that are traditional with this metal, and because of that fact it appeals to dealers with a discriminating clientele.

"B" illustrates the new "Fontaine" pattern, a unique single plate etching on both the new "Twilite" (evening blue) glass, and crystal with green trim. The new "Twilite" glass was one of the distinctive offerings at the January Show. The delicacy of this coloring, and the charming effect produced when used with the new tinted table cloths, reveal unusual sales possibilities.

"C" is the Flanders pattern, only a few months old but familiar to almost every glassware dealer.

"D"—This goblet, whose single plate etching is patterned after an old French motif, is the "Empire" on rose pink glass.

"E" is a cutting known as the "Willow" pattern.. It represents a style of decoration that is becoming more and more popular, and for which the United States Glass Co. has exceptional facilities. The goblet photographed is crystal with green trim. The buds at the top of the cutting are polished.

Another contribution of the United States Glass Co. this year is the "Old Gold" color in Tiffinware. "Old Gold" is having a very warm reception from the trade. Its beauty is revealed in the attractive line of pressed Tiffinware, comprising a score of quick-selling items that retail for about one dollar." The same line is also furnished in the new "Twilite."

Other new items of pressed Tiffinware are a bamboo-optic iced tea set, a smaller size of the handled flower basket which sold so well last year, a line of pink satin items with "Morning Glory" and "Autumn" decorations, and an assortment of crystal in the new Puritan pattern.

A departure from the traditional night set is a new "Room Set," consisting of a plump little pitcher with a tumbler that fits into the top instead of over it, and a convenient tray—in both pink and green .

Tiffinware advertising in the magazines during 1928, it is announced, will feature such patterns as the "Fontaine," "Empire," "Flanders," "Moritz," "Willow," "Classic," and others for which there is a steady and growing demand in open stock. In addition, both of the new colors—"Twilite" and "Old Gold"—will be shown.

D URING the last two years, the United States Glass Co. has been making a careful study of the tastes and desires of women in household glassware of various kinds. The success of the "Flanders" pattern in "Tiffinware," which was put on the market for the first time last year, and a very gratifying demand from all parts of the country for their new "Tiffinware" patterns and items displayed at the recent Pittsburgh Show would indicate that the United States Glass Co. has struck a responsive chord among users of glassware.

The goblets pictured here reveal the smartness and character of the patterns in five of the new "Tiffinware" lines.

"A" is an unusually attractive creation in rock crystal known as the "Moritz" pattern. The goblet is ten inches

Rose Pink #2, 8" h. Vase; #7, 9 1/4" h. Vase; #15033, Cocktail, Goblet, Wine. All Wide Optic. $275-325, $275-325, $30-40, $35-45, $30-40

Twilite: #032, 9 oz. Table Tumbler; #15033 Cocktail, Goblet, Wine, Saucer Champagne; #8869, Cup and Saucer. Twilite with Crystal trim #15033, Cordial, Sundae. All Wide Optic. $35-45, $40-50, $45-55, $40-50, $40-50, $75-100 set, $125-150, $40-50

Twilite #8814, 6" Plate; #8818, 10" Plate; #8833, 8" Plate; #345, 10" Handled Cake Plate. $15-25,$125-150, $20-30, $200-250

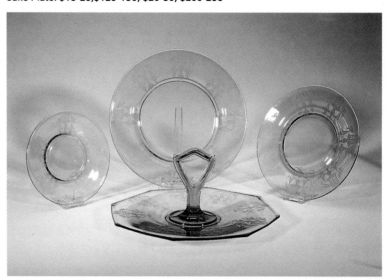

Twilite #9758, 5" Low Candlesticks; #8153, 13" Centerpiece Bowl. $200-250 pair, $150-200

Twilite #4, Sugar and Cream, Wide Optic. $200-250 set

Floris

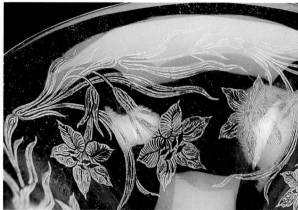

Detail of Floris etching.

Crystal with Green trim #004, 6" h. blown Comport, Wide Optic. $60-85

Twilite #032, 9 oz. Table Tumbler; #14194, Jug with cover. Both Wide Optic. $35-45, $550-650

Fuchsia

Crystal: #15083, Table Tumbler, Ice Tea, Cocktail, Saucer Champagne; #14196, Oyster Cocktail; #15083, Goblet; #5250, Mitrovich Cocktail; #15083, Cordial, Table Tumbler, Sundae, Café Parfait, Wine, Seltzer. All Wide Optic. $20-30, $20-30, $20-30, $20-30, $15-25,$25-35, $75-100, $45-55, $20-30, $20-30, $30-40, $25-35, $15-25

Crystal #15083, 10 oz. Goblet, Wide Optic. $25-35

Crystal: 12" h. Chinese Hurricane Shades, unknown line number; #526, 5 1/4" Medium Rose Bowl. $450-500 pair, $150-200

Crystal #17453, Ice Tea, Goblet, Cocktail. $25-35, $30-40, $25-35

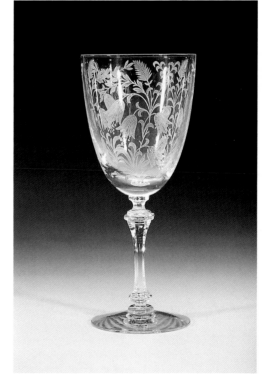

Crystal #17453, Goblet. $30-40

67

Top: Crystal: #5902, 12 1/2", 3-Part Relish; #8897, 12 1/4" 5-Part Relish; #8896, 9 3/4", 3-Part Relish. $55-75, $55-75, $45-65

Bottom: Crystal: #179, 12" Centerpiece Bowl; 11 1/4" Centerpiece Bowl with 8 crimps, unknown line number; 14 1/2" square Centerpiece Bowl, unknown line number. $65-85, $75-100, $75-100

Top: Crystal: #13872, 7 oz. Hi Ball Sham, Wide Optic; #450, 2 1/2" oz. Whiskey Sham; #517, 10 oz. Medium Sham Tumbler. $50-75, $75-100, $50-75

Bottom: Crystal #5902, 12 1/2" Flared Centerpiece Bowl, 12" Crimped Centerpiece Bowl, 10" Salad Bowl. $65-85, $75-100, $75-100

Top: Crystal: #15082, 6" Comport; #5831, 6 1/4" Tall Comport, #2, Salt and Pepper, Wide Optic. $75-100, $65-85, $125-150 pair

Bottom: Crystal: 2-Lite Candelabra: #15360, 7"; #5902, 7 1/2"; unknown line number, 9"; #5831, 7". $65-85, $65-85, $75-100, $55-75

Top: Crystal: #5902, Sugar and Cream, 6" Nut Bowl, 6 1/2" 3-Part Relish, 7" Nappy, 10 1/2" Celery Tray; #15082, 11" Bud Vase; #14185, 10", 8", 6" Bud Vases. $45-65 pair, $25-35, $25-35, $25-35, $55-75, $75-100, $40-50, $35-45, $30-40

Bottom: Crystal #5831: Mayonnaise set; 6" Handled Nappy; 12" Handled Cake Plate; 7 3/4" Handled Plate. $45-65 set, $40-50, $65-85, $45-65

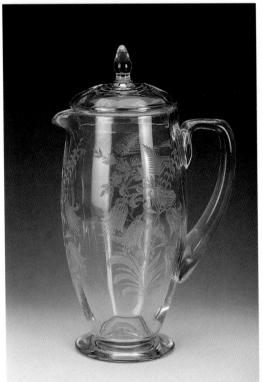

Top left: Crystal #15144 1/2, 11 1/4" h. Handled Vases. The entire vase is a pressed piece. $150-200 each

Top right: Crystal #128, 2 qt. Jug. $300-375

Bottom left: Crystal #14194, 2 qt. Jug with cover, Wide Optic. $300-375

Bottom center: Crystal with Ruby Stain #14185, 10 1/4" h. Bud Vases, gold inlay. $75-100 each

Center right: Detail of Fuchsia etching.

Hawe

Top left: Mandarin #075, 6 1/4" Handled Comport. $40-65

Top right: Detail of Hawe etching.

Helena

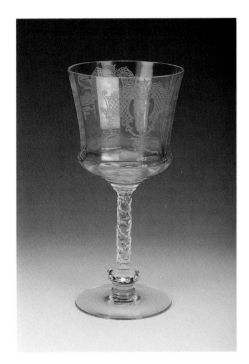

Above: Mandarin with Crystal trim #15066, Goblet, Wide Optic. $25-35

Right: *China, Glass, and Lamps,* December 26, 1927.

Isabella

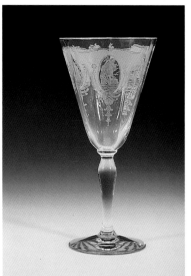

Crystal: #14187, Sundae, Goblet; #517 Handled Tumbler; #14187 Wine; #14185, Ice Tea; #517, Ice Tea; #14185, 2 qt. Covered Jug; #14187 Saucer Champagne. All Wide Optic. The jug cover is also etched Isabella. The blank for the #14185 jug is known as the Gothic jug. $25-35, $30-40, $40-50, $30-40, $25-35, $25-35, $400-500, $25-35

Top: Crystal #14187, Goblet, Wide Optic. $30-40

Bottom: Detail of Isabella etching.

Jap Lily

Julia

Top left: Crystal #14179, Goblet. $15-25

Top center: Crystal 8" Trumpet Vase, cut stem and star foot. $50-75

Crystal with Amber trim #15071, Cordial, Wide Optic. $75-100

Detail of Julia etching.

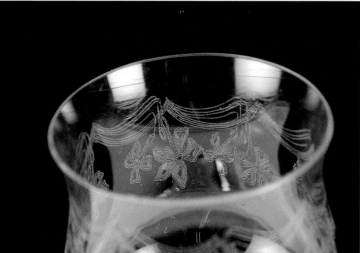

Detail of Jap Lily etching.

Crystal with Amber trim, Wide Optic: #14185, Ice Tea; #15011, Saucer Champagne, Cocktail, Wine, Goblet, Café Parfait, Cordial; #14194, 2 qt. Jug with cover; #14185, Table Tumbler, Seltzer; #6, Sugar and Cream. $30-40, $30-40, $30-40, $35-45, $35-45, $40-50, $75-100, $325-375, $30-40, $25-35, $125-175 pair

Juno

Topaz #348, 4" Candleholders. $45-65 pair

Lace

Bottom center: Crystal with Blue trim: #14185, 10" h. Bud Vase; #14185, Table Tumbler. Crystal with Amber trim #14185, 2 qt. Jug. An etched lid sometimes accompanies the jug. $65-85, $20-30, $300-375

Right: Detail of Lace etching.

La Fleure

Mandarin with Crystal trim #15024: Cordial, Goblet, Saucer Champagne, Cocktail; #5831, 10" Celery Tray. All Wide Optic. $75-100, $35-45, $30-40, $30-40, $50-70

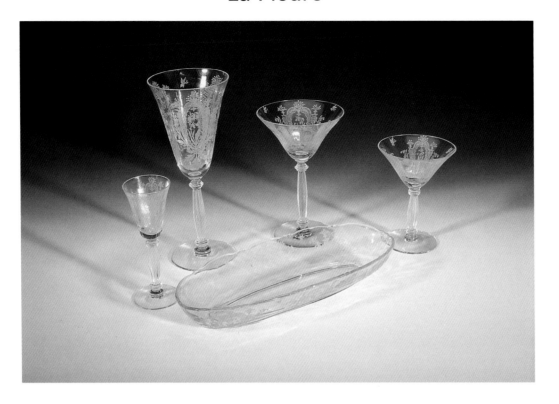

Right: Crystal #15024, Cordial, Wide Optic. $65-85

Center: Rose Pink with Crystal trim #15024, Saucer Champagne, Wide Optic. $25-35

Detail of La Fleure etching.

La Salle

Detail of La Salle etching.

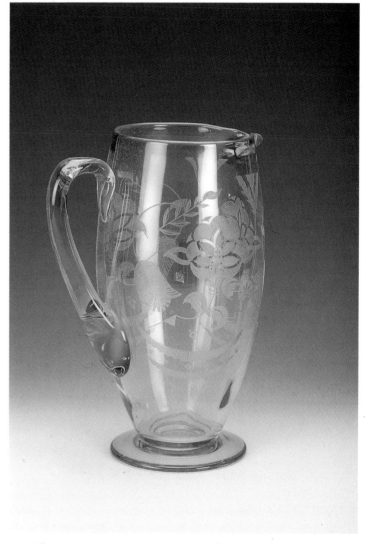

Crystal with Mandarin trim #15070, Goblet, Wide Optic. $30-40

Mandarin #14194, 2 qt. Jug, Wide Optic. $250-300

Luciana

Crystal with Nile Green trim: #14194, 2 qt. Jug with cover; #15016, Goblet; #004, 10 1/2" h. Bud Vase; #6, Cream and Sugar. Crystal with Black trim #15043, Wine. All Wide Optic. $400-500 $40-50, $125-150, $150-200 set, $30-40

Bottom left: Crystal with Nile Green trim #15016, Goblet, Wide Optic. $40-50

Center: Detail of Luciana etching.

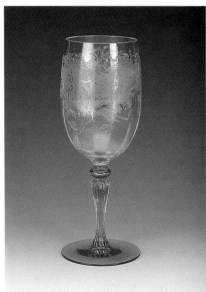

Crystal with Black trim #15037, Saucer Champagne, Wide Optic. Luciana is not usually found on the #15037 stem. $40-50

78

Melrose

FACTORY "R" TIFFIN, OHIO.
United States Glass Company, Pittsburgh, Pa., U. S. A.
GOLD ENC. "MELROSE" INLAID.
(Wide Optic) Crystal—Green Trim.

018-10 oz
Goblet.

018-6½ oz.
Sau. Champ.

018   Sundae

018 Cafe
Parfait

018-4½ oz.
Claret

018-3 oz.
Wine

018-3 oz.
Cocktail

Note: For complete itemization of this line,
see other side.

8833-8" Plate
(Not Optic) All Green.

185.   Ftd. Finger
Bowl.

018-9 oz.
Table.

194-2 Qt. Jug
and Cover.

6 Sugar

6 Cream

9557-½ lb.
Candy Jar and Cover.

Plate 765-018 Melrose Inlaid.

United States Glass Company catalog page featuring the Melrose plate etching with gold inlay.

Top left: Crystal with Reflex Green trim #15018: Goblet, Wine, Saucer Champagne. All Wide Optic with gold inlay and Melrose gold band. $75-100 each

Top center: Crystal with Reflex Green trim #15018, Goblet, Wide Optic, with gold inlay and Melrose gold band. $75-100

Top right: Crystal: #13633, Cordial; #14179, 1 qt. Decanter, faceted stopper. Both with Melrose gold band. $55-75, $275-325

Bottom left: Crystal: #15020, Table Tumbler; #13633, Cordial; Table Tumbler, unknown line number; #15020, Whiskey. All with Wide Optic and Melrose gold band. $25-35, $55-75, $25-35, $45-65

Bottom center: Detail of Melrose etching.

China, Glass, and Lamps, September 6, 1926.

China, Glass, and Lamps, 1926.

Amber: #14194, Jug with cover; #15020, Table Tumbler. Both with Wide Optic and Melrose gold band.

Crystal: #17356, Wine, Goblet, Cordial, Saucer Champagne; #14185, 10 1/4" h. Bud Vase. All Wide Optic with Melrose gold band. $75-100, $75-100, $100-125, $75-100, $65-85

Modernistic

Navarre

Nymph

TIFFIN *ware*

for ⊤ 1932

*M*ANY new things in Tiffin-ware are ready, including the handsome No. 068 shape in new decorations.

In quality pressed tableware, we announce the exquisite "Wakefield" This is a pure Colonial design of un-deniable beauty and suitable for hotels and restaurants as well as homes.

An attractive square stem features this No. 068 stemware line. Available in a choice of colors and combinations.

SEE ALL THE NEW LINES

Suite 869, 870, 871 and 872—Fort Pitt Hotel

Pittsburgh Exhibit—January 11th to 21st.

A Visit to Our Display Will be of Real Interest

UNITED STATES GLASS COMPANY

PITTSBURGH   PENNA.

A *China, Glass, and Lamps,* January, 1932, advertisement announcing the new #15068 stemline. The Navarre etching appears on the goblet.

Crystal with Nile Green trim #15011, Goblet, Wide Optic. $35-45

Detail of Nymph etching.

A January, 1927, *China, Glass, and Lamps* advertisement documenting the Nymph plate etching.

Opposite page:
Green #14185, 2 qt. Jug, Ice Tea. Both Wide Optic. $250-300, $20-30

Detail of Modernistic etching.

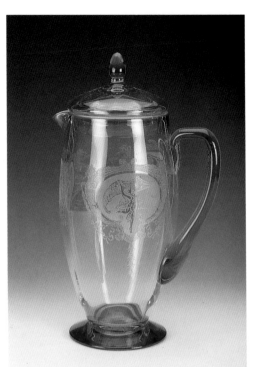

Crystal with Nile Green trim
#14194, 2 qt. Jug with cover,
Wide Optic. $400-500

Crystal with Nile Green trim: #15011,
Saucer Champagne, Sundae, Goblet,
Cocktail; #14185, Ice Tea. All Wide
Optic. $35-45, $35-45, $40-50, $35-45,
$35-45

Crystal with Reflex Green trim
#9557, ½ lb. Candy Jar and cover,
Wide Optic. $125-150

84

Oneida

Crystal: #348, 4" Candleholders; #348, 11" Centerpiece Bowl. Both with Green enameled etching. $50-75 pair, $45-65

Crystal: #348, 12" Handled Cake Plate; #319, 10" h. 2-handled Vase. Both with Blue enameled etching. $45-65, $75-100

Oneida

Persian Pheasant

Poppy

Crystal #17358, Goblet, Wide Optic. $25-35

Persian Pheasant

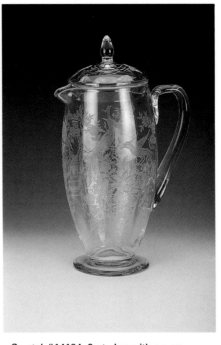

Crystal #14194, 2 qt. Jug with cover, Wide Optic. $300-350

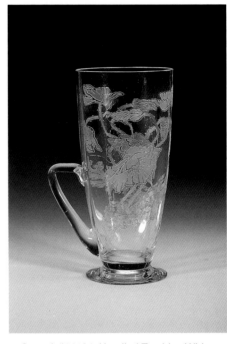

Crystal #14194, Handled Tumbler, Wide Optic. $35-45

Opposite page:
Top left: Crystal #13643, Cocktails, Wide Optic. $15-25

Top right: Crystal: #114, 3 pt. Tall Jug; #2, 10" h. Vase; #13643, Handled Sherbet; #133, Jug, cut neck. All Wide Optic. $125-175, $65-85, $15-25, $125-175

Bottom left: Crystal #13541, 1 qt. Decanter, cut neck, Wide Optic. $100-150

Bottom center: Crystal #13541, 1 qt. Decanter with stopper removed. The stopper, which has a large bubble, is made in the same general shape as the decanter.

Bottom right: Crystal: 5 3/4" h. Comport, 9" h. Comport, 5 3/4" h. Comport, unknown line numbers; #2, Almond Cups. $35-45, $40-50, $35-45, $15-25 each

Princess

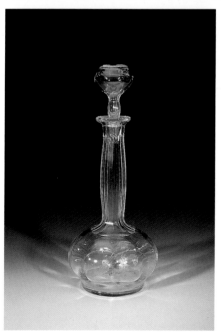

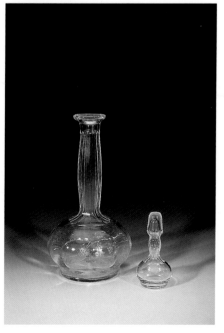

Psyche

Crystal with Nile Green trim: #15016, Saucer Champagne, Sundae, Goblet, Wine, Café Parfait; #14185, Finger Bowl; #14194 2 qt. Jug with cover; #15016, Cordial; #14194, Ice Tea. All Wide Optic. $35-45, $35-45, $40-50, $40-50, $45-55, $40-50, $400-500, $125-150, $35-40

Crystal with Nile Green trim #15016, Goblet, Wide Optic. $40-50

Detail of Psyche etching.

Above: Crystal with Nile Green trim #15003, Café Parfait, Cocktail. Both with cased "button," Wide Optic. $50-60 each

Above right: Crystal #15039, Cocktail, Wide Optic. $25-35

Right: *China, Glass, and Lamps,* 1926.

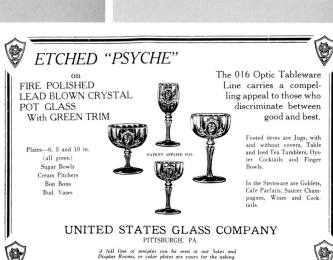

Queen Astrid

Rosalind

Detail of Rosalind etching.

Opposite page:
Top left: Crystal #17351, Goblet. $25-35

Top center: Crystal #17351, Goblet, Saucer Champagne, Ice Tea. $25-35, $20-30, $20-30

Top right: Crystal 2-Lite, 9" Candelabra, unknown line number. $75-100 pair.

Bottom left: Queen Astrid

Bottom center: Crystal: #14185, 10 1/4" h. Bud Vase; #9742, Table Bell; #14185, 6" h. Bud Vase. $35-45, $45-65, $30-40

Bottom right: Crystal: #17311, 4", Cigarette Box and cover; #17311, 4" Ash Trays. The #17311 ash tray is listed as an individual salt or ash tray. $30-40, $20-30 each

Rose Marie

Mandarin #15042, Saucer Champagne, Goblet, Sundae. All Wide Optic. $20-30, $25-35, $20-30

China, Glass, and Lamps, March 1930, advertisement announcing the introduction of the Rosalind etching and the #15042 stemline. Note that the colors Rose Pink and Mandarin are now identified as DuBarry Rose and Mandarin Gold.

Rose Marie.

Crystal #310, 11" Open Work Fruit Bowl. $45-65

Roses

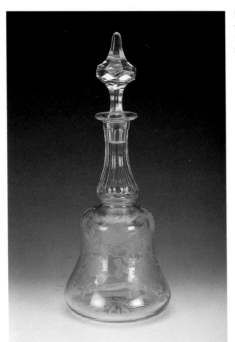

Crystal #14179, 30 oz. Decanter, cut neck, faceted stopper. $175-225

Roses.

Special Thistle

Crystal #14197, Cordial, Wide Optic. $40-65

Crystal #6712, Night Cap Set, Wide Optic. $65-85 set

Crystal #6712, Night Cap Set, with tumbler removed.

Crystal #983, 1 qt. Decanter, cut neck, faceted stopper. $150-200

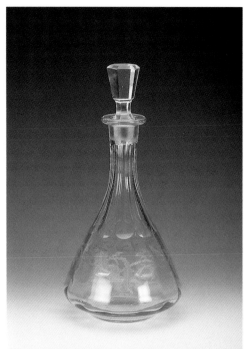

Crystal: #13882, 22 oz. Grape Fruit and Liner; #13891, 20 oz. Grape Fruit and Liner; #13882, 22 oz. Grape Fruit and Liner. All Wide Optic. $50-70, $45-65, $50-70

Crystal #14153, 6" Low Bon Bon. $45-65

93

Thistle

Tourainne

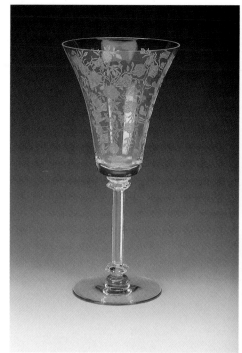
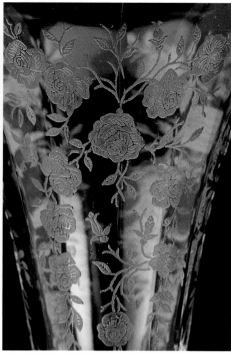

Vintage

Top left: Crystal #14180, 9 oz. Goblet, Wide Optic. $15-25

Top left center: Crystal: #354, 7 oz. Tumbler, Wide Optic; #104, 2 qt. Jug, star bottom. $15-25, $125-175

Top right center: Crystal #17328, Goblet, Wide Optic. $20-30

Top right: Detail of Tourainne etching.

Bottom left: Crystal #14180, 9 oz. Goblet, Wide Optic. $20-30

Bottom center: Detail of Vintage etching.

Bottom right: Canary #4, Cream; Blue with Canary trim #14196, Goblet. Both Wide Optic. $45-55, $30-40

Wallpaper

Detail of Wallpaper etching.

Crystal with Reflex
Green trim #14185,
Table Tumbler. $25-35

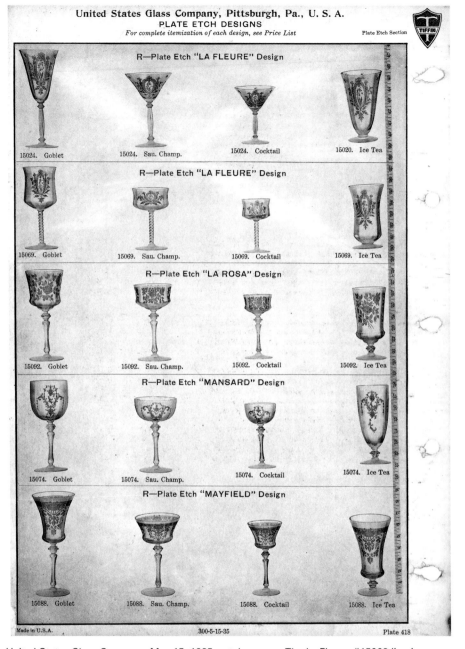

United States Glass Company, February 2, 1936, catalog page documenting the previously unknown Arbor and Lacette plate etchings, and the Regent gold or platinum band.

United States Glass Company, May 15, 1935, catalog page. The La Fleure #15069 line is a previously undocumented stemline for this pattern. The La Rosa and Mayfield plate etchings are also previously unidentified etchings produced at Factory R.

Chapter 3: Engravings

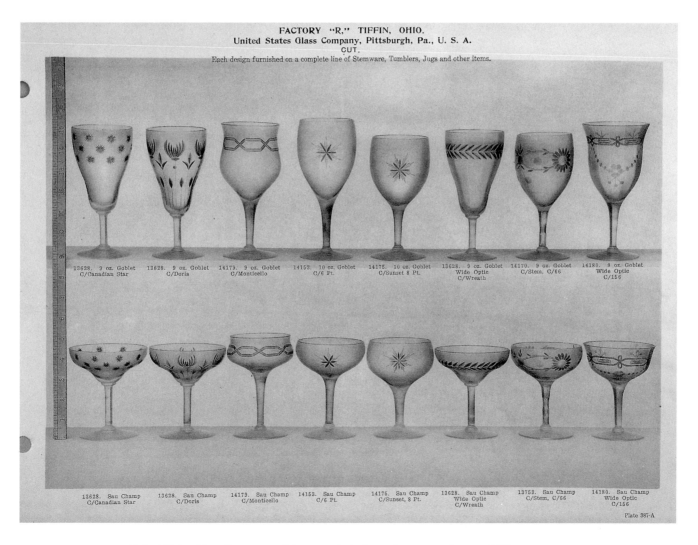

13628. 9 oz. Goblet
C/Canadian Star

13628. 9 oz. Goblet
C/Doris

14179. 9 oz. Goblet
C/Monticello

14153. 10 oz. Goblet
C/6 Pt.

14175. 10 oz. Goblet
C/Sunset 8 Pt.

13628. 9 oz. Goblet
Wide Optic
C/Wreath

14170. 9 oz. Goblet
C/Stem, C/66

14180. 9 oz. Goblet
Wide Optic
C/156

13628. Sau Champ
C/Canadian Star

13628. Sau Champ
C/Doris

14179. Sau Champ
C/Monticello

14153. Sau Champ
C/6 Pt.

14175. Sau Champ
C/Sunset, 8 Pt.

13628. Sau Champ
Wide Optic
C/Wreath

13753. Sau Champ
C/Stem, C/66

14180. Sau Champ
Wide Optic
C/156

Plate 387-A

United States Glass Company catalog page featuring various engravings, c. 1920.

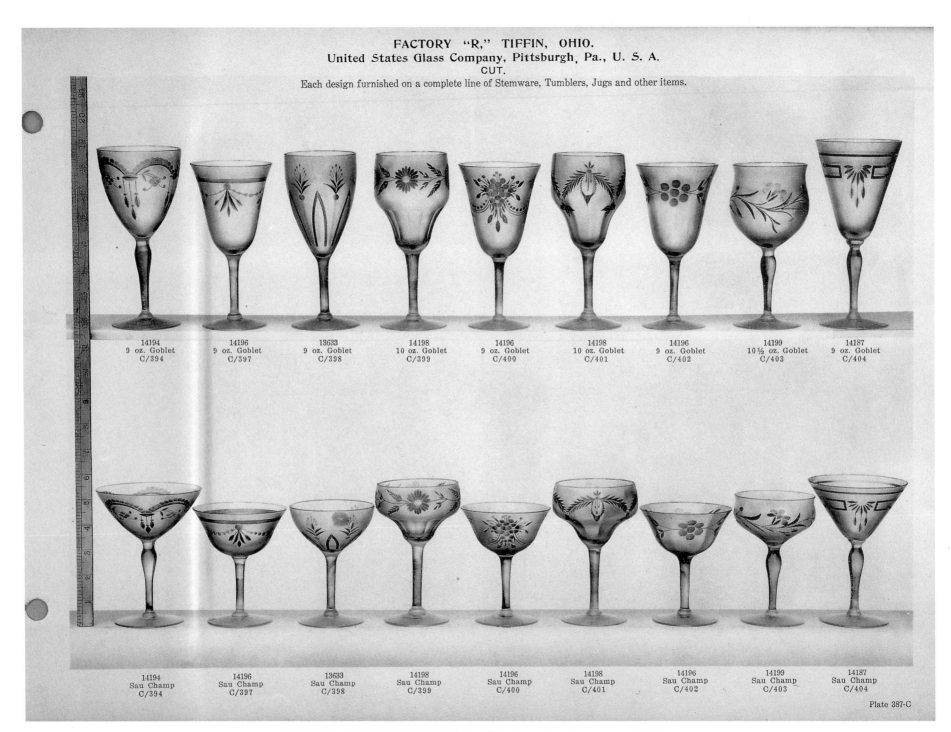

14194	14196	13633	14198	14196	14198	14196	14199	14187
9 oz. Goblet	9 oz. Goblet	9 oz. Goblet	10 oz. Goblet	9 oz. Goblet	10 oz. Goblet	9 oz. Goblet	10½ oz. Goblet	9 oz. Goblet
C/394	C/397	C/398	C/399	C/400	C/401	C/402	C/403	C/404

14194	14196	13633	14198	14196	14198	14196	14199	14187
Sau Champ	Sau Champ	Sau Champ	Sau Champ	Sau Champ	Sau Champ	Sau Champ	Sau Champ	Sau Champ
C/394	C/397	C/398	C/399	C/400	C/401	C/402	C/403	C/404

Plate 387-C

United States Glass Company catalog page featuring various engravings, c. 1920.

98

8177. Centerpiece Set
Cut "Clinton" Design

8177. Centerpiece Set
Cut "Clinova" Design

8177. Centerpiece Set
Dec. "Dickson" Design

This April, 1933, United States Glass Company catalog page illustrates the previously undocumented Clinton and Clinova engravings. The Dickson design is an enameled etching.

Cut #360 Design (Cut Butterfly)

Cut #360 Design

A popular pattern from the early 1920s, cut #360 features a butterfly engraving. A wide selection of items was offered in Crystal on stemline #14178, selected items were available in Green.

Above: Crystal: #14178, Goblet, Wine, Sundae, Saucer Champagne; #19, 10" h. Bud Vase; #14153, 8" Deep Comport; #3 Sugar and Cream; #5714, 7" h. French Dressing Bottle; #107, qt. Jug; #14179, 5 1/2" h. Oil Bottle; #451, 9 oz. Tumbler. $10-20, $15-25, $10-20, $10-20, $40-50, $50-70, $45-65, $45-65, $125-175, $55-75, $10-20

Top right: Crystal #14178, Goblet. $15-25

Right: Detail of #360 cut design.

Cut #405 Design (Double Columbine)

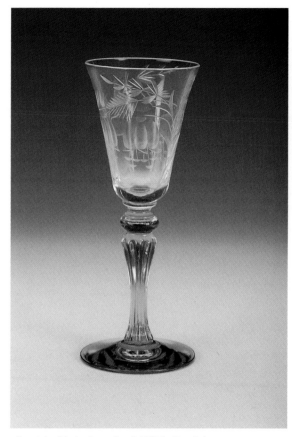

Crystal with Amber trim #15071, Cordial, Wide Optic. $55-75

Crystal with Amber trim: #15071, Saucer Champagne, Cordial; #14185, Ice Tea, Table Tumbler; #14194, 2 qt. Jug. All Wide Optic. $20-30, $55-75, $20-30, $15-20, $200-250

Cut #405 Design

    Cut #405 Design, commonly known as "Double Columbine" by collectors was offered in Crystal or Rose on stemline #15037, and in Crystal with Amber trim, and Crystal with Green trim on stemline #15011. This design was available c. 1930. A similar engraving, cut #424 Design, was offered in Mandarin on stemline #15042, and is known as "Single Columbine."

011—9 oz.
Goblet.
$21.00

011. Sml. Sau.
Champ. $21.00

011. Sml. Sundae
$20.50

011. Cafe
Parfait
$21.00

011. Claret
$20.50

011—3 oz.
Wine
$19.50

011—3 oz.
Cocktail
$19.50

185. Ftd. Finger
Bowl, $27.00

THE MERIDEN GRAVURE CO.

185—8½ oz.
Ftd. Table, $18.90
Also furnish Ftd.
Seltzer, $18.00 and
Ftd. Ice Tea, $21.00

194—2 Qt. Jug and Cover,
$84.00. Also furnish
without Cover, $72.00

No. 6. Sugar
$31.20

No. 6. Cream
$28.00

9557—½ lb.
Candy Jar and Cover.
$40.50

8833—8 in. Salad Plate (Not Opt.) $37.50
Also furnish
8814—6 in. $24.00 and 8835—10 in. $45.00
Plate 365—405 Green Trim.

United States Glass Company catalog page featuring cut #405 design, commonly known by collectors as "Double Columbine."

102

Doris

Green Wheat

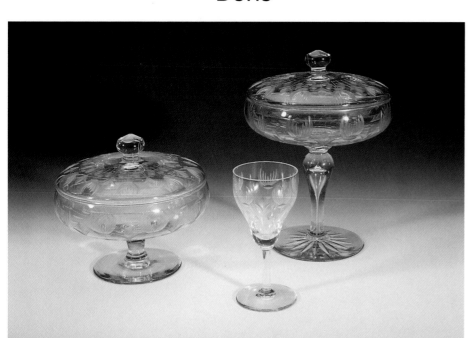

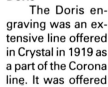
Top left: Crystal: #14153, 6" Low Foot Bon Bon and cover, cut finial; #13628, 2 oz. Wine; #9556, 7 3/4" h. High Foot Bon Bon and cover, cut finial, bubble stem. All Wide Optic. $60-80, $15-25, $75-100

Bottom left: *China, Glass, and Lamps,* 1922.

Doris

The Doris engraving was an extensive line offered in Crystal in 1919 as a part of the Corona line. It was offered in the Corona stemline #0211, which was later renumbered #13628. Selected items in this line are the #9551 hair receiver, #9560 syrup jug, #9551 puff box with cover, #9557 candy jar in ½ lb. and 1 lb. sizes, and the #91-5 1 qt. grape juice jug.

Green Wheat

The Green Wheat engraving was offered on stemline #15039 in Crystal with Green trim. The design is a gray cutting of sprays cut in four different lengths, with no color on the engraving.

Cut #394 Design

Cut #387 Design

Crystal: #13633, 2 ½ oz. Wines;
#14194, 1 qt. Tall Covered Tankard.
$15-25 each, $175-225

Detail of cut #394 design.

Cut #394 Design

Introduced in 1924, cut #394 Design was offered on stemline #14194 in Crystal. The extensive
line included 1 qt. and 2 qt. #14194 jugs, #14194 oil
bottle, #5714 French dressing bottle, and a 1 lb.
#9557 candy jar.

Cut #387 Design

An early 1920s floral engraving, cut #387 was
produced in Crystal on stemline #14153. Offerings
included #117 and #112 2 qt. jugs, #9261 large marmalade, and the #9556 high foot bon bon.

Crystal #9557, 1 lb. Large Candy
Jar and cover, Wide Optic. The
#9557 ½ lb. Candy jar is the
common size. The #9557 1 lb. is
considered scarce. $75-100

Unidentified Engravings

Crystal with Canary trim: #14185, Table Tumblers; #14194, 2 qt. Jug. All Wide Optic, unknown engraving. $15-25 each, $200-250

Bottom left: Crystal with Nile Green trim: #14185, Ice Tea; #15001, Goblet, Sundae; #14194, Jug with cover. All Wide Optic, unknown engraving. $15-25, $20-30, $15-25, $200-250

Center: Crystal with Nile Green trim #15016, Goblet, Saucer Champagne. All Wide Optic, unknown engraving. $25-35, $20-30

Crystal with Blue trim: #4, Sugar and Cream; #14194, 2 qt. Jug with cover, unknown engraving. Both Wide Optic. $100-125 set, $200-250

Chapter 4: Corona Line

The Corona line catalog was issued in 1919 by the United States Glass Company. The catalog promoted an assortment of cuttings, needle and plate etchings, and sand blast designs produced at Factory R, Tiffin, Ohio. Included were crystal jugs, decanters, vases, tumblers, stemware, marmalades, nappies and baskets. Two known Heisey Glass Company basket blanks were offered with Tiffin Glass cuttings, the #0361 8" basket and the #0362 9" basket. The Heisey diamond H mark appears on the bottom of these baskets.

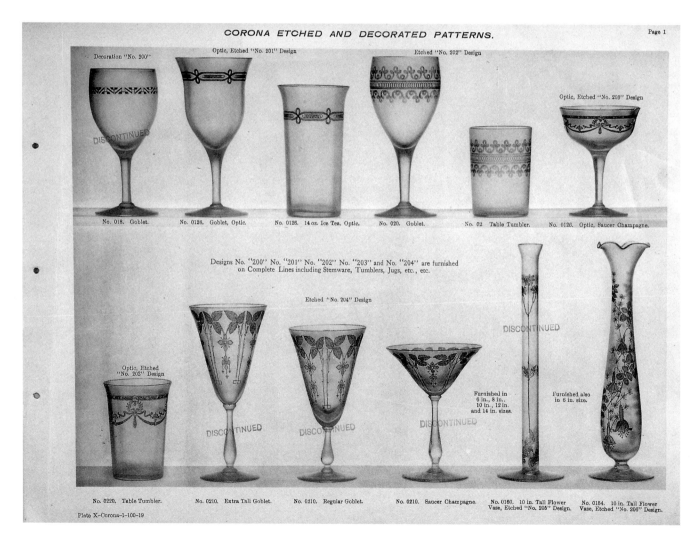

CORONA ETCHED AND DECORATED PATTERNS.

Page 1

Decoration "No. 200"   Optic, Etched "No. 201" Design   Etched "No. 202" Design   Optic, Etched "No. 203" Design

No. 018. Goblet.   No. 0126. Goblet, Optic.   No. 0126. 14 oz. Ice Tea, Optic.   No. 020. Goblet.   No. 02. Table Tumbler.   No. 0126. Optic, Saucer Champagne.

Designs No. "200" No. "201" No. "202" No. "203" and No. "204" are furnished on Complete Lines including Stemware, Tumblers, Jugs, etc., etc.

Etched "No. 204" Design

Optic, Etched "No. 203" Design

Furnished in 6 in., 8 in., 10 in., 12 in. and 14 in. sizes.

Furnished also in 6 in. size.

No. 0220. Table Tumbler.   No. 0210. Extra Tall Goblet.   No. 0210. Regular Goblet.   No. 0210. Saucer Champagne.   No. 0160. 10 in. Tall Flower Vase, Etched "No. 205" Design.   No. 0154. 10 in. Tall Flower Vase, Etched "No. 206" Design.

Plate X-Corona-1-100-19

CORONA GOBLETS.

Complete Lines of Stemware, Tumblers, Jugs, etc.,
are furnished in each of these Patterns.

DISCONTINUED

DISCONTINUED

No. 018. Goblet.
Border.

No. 018. Saucer Champagne.
Border.

No. 018. Goblet.
6 Point Star.

No. 018. Goblet.
Catawba.

No. 018. Goblet.
Sunburst.

No 018. Goblet.
Vineland.

No. 018. Goblet.
Anna.

No. 020. Goblet.
Dart.

No. 018. Goblet.
Simplicity.

Plate X—Corona-2-100–19

107

CORONA GOBLETS.

Complete Lines of Stemware, Tumblers, Jugs, etc.,
are furnished in each of these Patterns.

Page 3

No. 018. Goblet.
Marie.

No. 020. Goblet.
Edna.

No. 020. Goblet.
Ellen.

No. 0126. Goblet.
Optic, Cut "156"

No. 0126. Goblet.
Virginia.

No. 0126. Goblet.
Optic, Cut "155"

No. 018. Goblet.
Cut "66"

No. 0211. Goblet.
Doris.

No. 020. Goblet.
Vivian.

No. 0126. Goblet.
Vera.

Plate X-Corona-3-100-19

Anna
No. 02.
9 oz. Table Tumbler.

Dart
DISCONTINUED
No. 04.
8 oz. Bell Tumbler.

Marie
No. 05.
8 oz. Bell Tumbler.
Sham Bottom.

Ellen
DISCONTINUED
No. 07.
3 oz. Whiskey Tumbler.
5 oz. Grape Juice Tumbler.

Virginia
DISCONTINUED
No. 07.
8 oz. High Ball
Tumbler.

66
No. 07.
10 oz. Table Tumbler.

Nan
DISCONTINUED
No. 07.
12 oz. Iced Tea Tumbler.

Vivian
DISCONTINUED
No. 0124.
14 oz. Iced Tea Tumbler.

Ruth
DISCONTINUED
No. 08. Tumbler.
8 oz. High Ball.
10 oz. Mineral.

Vera
DISCONTINUED
No. 08. Tumbler.
12 oz. Iced Tea.
14 oz. Iced Tea.

Anna
No. 09.
2½ oz. Whiskey.
3 oz. Whiskey.

Dart
DISCONTINUED
No. 09. Tumbler.
5 oz. Grape Juice.

Marie
No. 09. Tumbler.
9 oz. Table.

Ellen
DISCONTINUED
No. 010.
12 oz. Handled Ice Tea.

Virginia
DISCONTINUED
No. 0111.
8 oz. Handled Ale.

66
No. 093.
Handled Footed Iced Tea.

Anna
No. 012. 2 Quart Jug.

Dart
DISCONTINUED
No. 014. 2 Quart Jug.
No. 0122. 1 Quart Jug.

Nan
DISCONTINUED
No. 011. 2 Quart Jug.

66
No. 015. 2 Quart Jug.

Vivian
DISCONTINUED
No. 017. 2 Quart Covered Jug.
No. 016. 2 Quart,
Same as No. 017, but without Cover.

109

Marie
No. 018 Goblet.

Anna
No. 018 Saucer Champagne.

"66"
No. 018 Sundae.

6 Pt. Star
No. 018 Claret.

Sunburst
No. 018 Sherry.

Catawba
No. 018 Wine.

Anna
No. 018 Cocktail.

Marie
No. 018 Creme de Menthe.

"66"
No. 018 Brandy.

Anna
No. 018 Cordial.

Vivian
No. 020 Goblet.

Ellen
No. 020 Saucer Champagne.

Dart
No. 020 Sundae.

Ellen
No. 020 Claret.

Dart
No. 020 Wine.

Ellen
No. 020 Sherry.

Vivian
No. 020 Cocktail.

Dart
No. 020 Brandy.

Ellen
No. 020 Cordial.

Virginia
No. 0126 Goblet.

Vera
No. 0126 Saucer Champagne.

Virginia
No. 0126 Sundae.

Vera
No. 0126 Claret.

Virginia
No. 0126 Sherry.

Vera
No. 0126 Wine.

Virginia
No. 0126 Creme de Menthe.

Virginia
No. 0126 Cocktail.

Vera
No. 0126 Brandy.

Virginia
No. 0126 Cordial.

Plate X-Corona-5-100-19

110

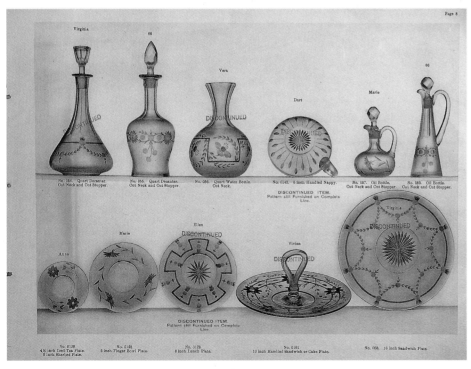

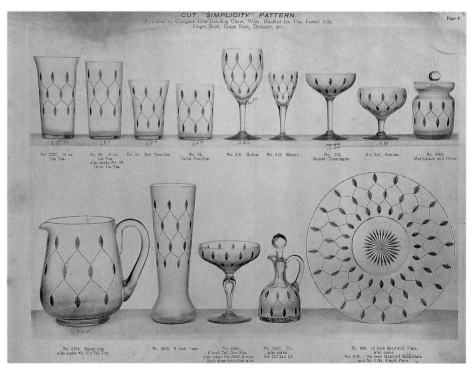

CUT "EDNA" PATTERN.

Furnished on Complete Line including Claret, Wine, Sherry, Ice Tea, Mineral, Whiskey and
Seltzer Tumblers, Footed Jelly, Oil, Sugar and Cream, Marmalade, Decanter, etc.

No. 0242. French Dressing Bottle.   No. 0225. 14 oz. Ice Tea.   No. 07. Table Tumbler.   No. 010. 12 oz. Ice Tea Handled. Also make without Handle.   No. 026. Goblet.   No. 090. Saucer Champagne.   No. 020. Cocktail.   No. 020. Sundae.   No. 027. Oyster Cocktail.

No. 0181. 10½ inch Handled Cake Plate. Also make No. 068. 10 inch Sandwich Plate and No. 0128. 6 inch Plate.   No. 0201. 10 inch Vase. Also make 8 inch.   No. 0253. 8 inch High Bon Bon. Also make No. 0252. 5 inch. Both sizes furnished with or without Covers.   No. 0273. Jug. Has Star Bottom and Beaded Top.   No. 017. Covered Jug. Has Star Bottom and Beaded Cover.

NO. 0126 LINE, OPTIC, CUT "156" PATTERN.

A pleasing combination of Cutting and Etching, furnished on
Wide Optic Lead Blown Blanks.

No. 0241. Oil.   Sundae.   No. 027. Oyster Cocktail.   Saucer Champagne.   Goblet.   No. 0124. Table Tumbler.   No. 0124. 11 oz. Lemonade.   No. 0124. 14 oz. Ice Tea Tumbler.

Furnished on Complete Line including Claret, Wine, Sherry, Cocktail,
Creme de Menthe, Cafe Parfait, Decanter, etc.

No. 087. Sugar and Cream.   No. 0340. Finger Bowl and No. 0128. 6 inch Plate.   No. 082. Low Grape Fruit.   No. 0253. 8 inch High Ftd. Bon Bon and Cover. Also make 6 in. Low. Ft. No. 040.   No. 011. 2 Quart Jug. Also make No. 0275 Tall Ice Jug and Cover.   Also made without Cover.

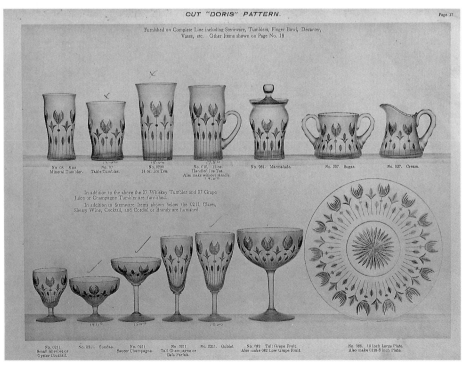

CUT "DORIS" PATTERN.

Furnished on Complete Line including Stemware, Tumblers, Finger Bowl, Decanter,
Vases, etc. Other Items shown on Page No. 18

No. 08. 8 oz. Mineral Tumbler.   No. 07. Table Tumbler.   No. 0226. 14 oz. Ice Tea.   No. 010. 12 oz. Handled Ice Tea. Also make without Handle.   No. 064. Marmalade.   No. 087. Sugar.   No. 037. Cream.

In addition to the above the 07 Whiskey Tumbler and 07 Grape
Juice or Champagne Tumbler are furnished.
In addition to Stemware Items shown below the 0211 Claret,
Sherry Wine, Cocktail, and Cordial or Brandy are furnished.

No. 0211. Small Sherbet or Oyster Cocktail.   No. 0211. Sundae.   No. 0211. Saucer Champagne.   No. 0211. Tall Champagne or Cafe Parfait.   No. 0211. Goblet.   No. 082. Tall Grape Fruit. Also make 082 Low Grape Fruit.   No. 068. 10 inch Large Plate. Also make 0128 6 inch Plate.

CUT "DORIS" PATTERN.

MISCELLANEOUS ITEMS.
See also Catalog Page No. 17

No. 040. 5 inch Low Footed Jelly.   No. 0253. 6 inch High Ftd. Bon Bon and Cover.   No. 0250. 4½ inch High Ftd. Bon Bon and Cover.   No. 040. 5 inch Low Ftd. Jelly and Cover.   No. 046. 5 inch Ftd. Almond or Low Comport and Cover.   No. 0406. Puff Box and Cover. Also make 0400 Hair Receiver. Same size.

These Items are also furnished without Covers.

No. 0410. 1 lb. Candy Jar and Cover. Also makes ½ lb. Size.   No. 0274. Squat Jug.   No. 0275. Tall Ice Tea Jug and Cover.   No. 0430. 12 in. Large Vase.   No. 0390. 10 in. Vase. Also make 8 inch.   No. 0420. Finger Bowl and No. 0128. Finger Bowl Plate.

Cut 97 — No. 078. Sugar.

Cut 150 — No. 078. Cream.

Cut Lattice — No. 078. Sugar.

Cut 100 — DISCONTINUED — No. 078. Cream.

Cut 108 — DISCONTINUED — No. 078. Sugar.

Cut 88 — No. 078. Cream.

Cut 110 — No. 078. Sugar.

Cut 111 — No. 078. Cream.

The Cuttings shown on above Sugars and Creams are also furnished on Bowls, Water Sets, Vases, etc.

No. 076. 8 inch Bowl. Cut 150. Has Star Bottom.

No. 076. 8 inch Bowl. Cut 110. Has Star Bottom and Beaded Top.

No. 079. 8 inch Bowl. Cut 111. Has Star Bottom and Beaded Top.

The Cuttings shown on Bowls, also furnished on Water Sets, Vases, Sugars and Creams, etc.

Plate X–Corona–21–100–19

Each Pattern also Furnished on other Shapes in Addition to those Illustrated.

No. 077. 13 inch.
Cut 97

No. 0195. 13 inch.
Cut Lattice

No. 0804. 12 inch.
Cut 150

No. 0807. 12 inch.
Cut 150

No. 0802. 13 inch. Large.
Cut 150

DISCONTINUED

DISCONTINUED

No. 0195. 12 inch.
Cut 100

No. 077. 12 inch.
Cut 108

No. 0196. 13 inch.
Cut 88

No. 0303. 12 inch. Heavy.
Cut 110

No. 0305. 13 inch. Large. Heavy.
Cut 111

Water Sets, Sugar and Cream Sets, and Bowls also Furnished in these Designs.

Plate X–Corona–22–100–19

All Jugs have Star Bottoms and Beaded Tops, all Tumblers are Star Bottom.
Each Cutting shown is Furnished on Both the Tall and Low Jugs.

No. 075. Tumbler.
Cut 97

No. 072. Jug.
Cut 97

No. 0221. Tumbler.
Cut 150

No. 0270. Jug.
Cut 150

No. 075. Tumbler.
Cut Lattice

No. 072. Jug.
Cut Lattice

No. 075. Tumbler.
Cut 100

No. 073. Jug.
Cut 100

Other Items such as Sugar and Cream Sets, Bowls, Vases, etc., are furnished in each of these Designs.

DISCONTINUED

DISCONTINUED

No. 075. Tumbler.
Cut 108

No. 072. Jug.
Cut 108

No. 075. Tumbler.
Cut 88

No. 073. Jug.
Cut 88

No. 075. Tumbler.
Cut 110

No. 072. Jug.
Cut 110

No. 075. Tumbler.
Cut 111

No. 073. Jug.
Cut 111

Plate X–Corona–23–100–19

CORONA BASKETS, CRACKER JARS AND MISCELLANEOUS ITEMS.

The Cut 150 Pattern furnished on Water Sets, Vases, Bowls, Sugars and Creams, etc.
The Cut Virginia Pattern furnished on Complete Line including Stemware.

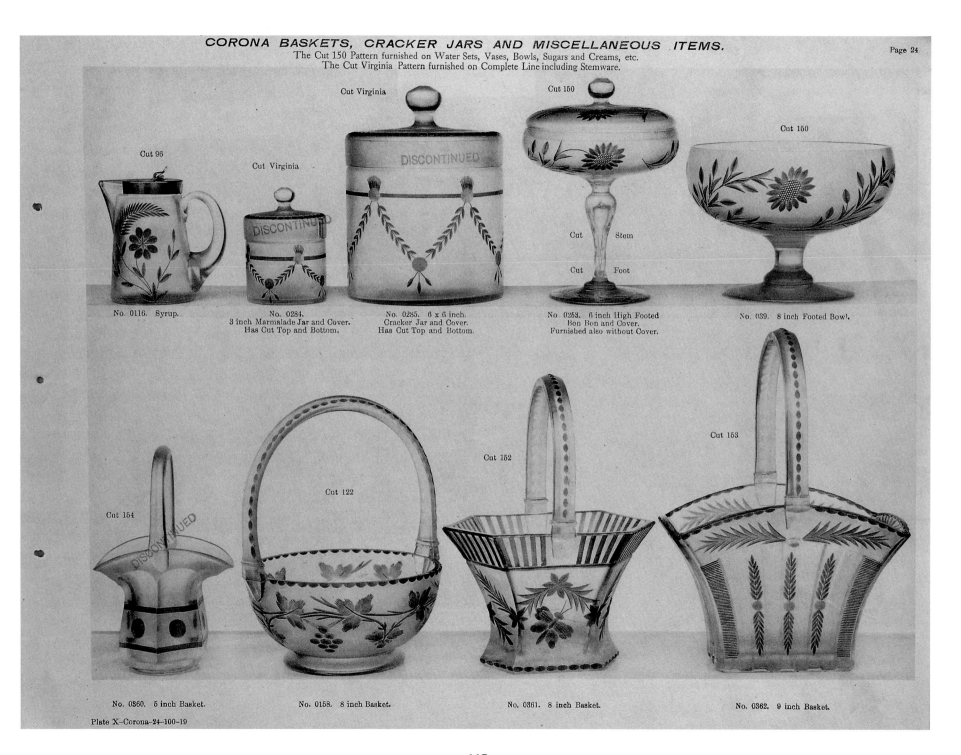

Cut 96

Cut Virginia

Cut Virginia

DISCONTINUED

Cut 150

DISCONTINUED

Cut 150

Cut Stem

Cut Foot

No. 0116. Syrup.

No. 0284.
3 inch Marmalade Jar and Cover.
Has Cut Top and Bottom.

No. 0285. 6 x 6 inch.
Cracker Jar and Cover.
Has Cut Top and Bottom.

No 0253. 6 inch High Footed
Bon Bon and Cover.
Furnished also without Cover.

No. 039. 8 inch Footed Bowl.

Cut 154

DISCONTINUED

Cut 122

Cut 152

Cut 153

No. 0360. 5 inch Basket.

No. 0158. 8 inch Basket.

No. 0361. 8 inch Basket.

No. 0362. 9 inch Basket.

Plate X-Corona-24-100-19

115

Water Goblets and other Tumblers also Furnished with each Design.

Cut "SIMPLICITY"   Cut "MARIE"   Cut "EDNA"

No 0220.
14 oz. Iced Tea.

No. 0275. Covered Jug.

No. 08.
12 oz. Iced Tea.

No. 08. 14 oz.
Iced Tea.

No. 0275. Covered Jug.
Has Star Bottom.

No. 010.
12 oz. Hld. Tumbler.

No. 07.
12 oz. Iced Tea.

No. 0275. Covered Jug.
Has Star Bottom.

No. 0220.
14 oz. Iced Tea.

Cut "ELLEN"   Etched "203" Optic.   Etched "204"

No. 08.
12 oz. Iced Tea.

No. 0275. Covered Jug.
Has Star Bottom.

No. 010. 12 oz.
Hld. Iced Tea.

No. 093.
12 oz. Hld. and
Ftd. Iced Tea.

No. 0220.
11 oz. Lemonade.

No. 0275. Covered Jug.
Has Star Bottom.

No. 0220. 14 oz.
Iced Tea.

No. 0220.
14 oz. Iced Tea.

No. 0275. Covered Jug.
Has Star Bottom.

No. 0220. 11 oz.
Lemonade.

Plate X-Corona-27-100-19.

All Designs shown are Furnished on the Regular Jug and the Covered Jug,
Also on either the 09-5 oz. Tumbler and the 09½-5 oz. Hld. Tumbler.

Cut Special Catawba   Cut Vineland   Cut Anna   Cut 66

No. 09½. 5 oz.   No. 0123. Covered Jug 1 qt.   No. 09. 5 oz.   No. 09½. 5 oz.   No. 0123. Covered Jug, 1 qt.   No. 09. 5 oz.   No. 09½. 5 oz.   No. 0123. Covered Jug, 1 qt.   No. 09. 5 oz.   No. 09½. 5 oz.   No. 0123. Covered Jug, 1 qt.   No. 09. 5 oz.

Cut Special Catawba   Cut Vineland   Cut Anna   Cut 66

No. 09½. 5 oz.   No. 0122. Jug, 1 qt.   No. 09. 5 oz.   No. 09½. 5 oz.   No. 0122. Jug, 1 qt.   No. 09. 5 oz.   No. 09½. 5 oz.   No. 0122. Jug, 1 qt.   No. 09. 5 oz.   No. 09½. 5 oz.   No. 0122. Jug, 1 qt.   No. 09. 5 oz.

Plate X–Corona–29–100–19

Chapter 5: Sand Blast Designs

The sand blast process was used to decorate crystal stemware and tableware lines from c. 1919-1935. A 1924 price listing included nine different designs. This style of decoration was popular for custom-designed orders. The sand blast procedure was not the same decorating process used to produce the sand-carved designs of the 1940s.

United States Glass Company catalog page featuring sand blast (emery cut) designs c. 1920.

A May 15, 1935, United States Glass Company catalog page showing three sand blast designs.

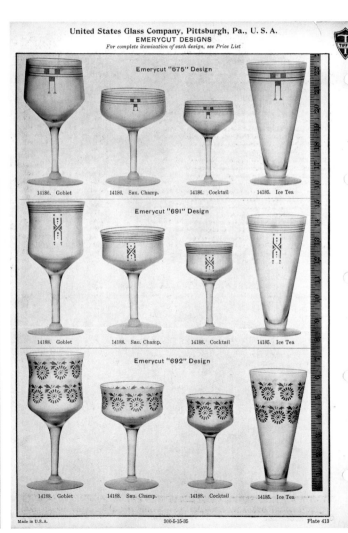

United States Glass Company, Pittsburgh, Pa., U. S. A.
EMERYCUT DESIGNS
For complete itemization of each design, see Price List

Emerycut "675" Design

14186. Goblet   14186. Sau. Champ.   14186. Cocktail   14185. Ice Tea

Emerycut "691" Design

14188. Goblet   14188. Sau. Champ.   14188. Cocktail   14185. Ice Tea

Emerycut "692" Design

14188. Goblet   14188. Sau. Champ.   14188. Cocktail   14185. Ice Tea

Made in U.S.A.   300-5-15-35   Plate 413

Crystal #14153, 3 oz. Wine, No. 675 sand blast design. $10-20

FACTORY "R," TIFFIN, OHIO.
United States Glass Company, Pittsburgh, Pa., U. S. A.
SAND BLAST.
Each design furnished on a complete line of Stemware, Tumblers, Jugs and other items.

Plate 1915-A

Chapter 6: Decorated and Plain Lines

Craquelle

The Craquelle decoration was achieved by immersing molten glass in cold water, which resulted in cracking the glass. The glass was then reheated and shaped. Craquelle ware was popular c. 1924. Production was limited to jugs and tumblers, which were marketed as ice tea sets.

Guild Gossamer

The Guild Gossamer line was designed by Rowena Reed Kostellow in 1938 for the United States Glass Company. Similar in appearance to Craquelle, the Guild Gossamer ware was hand-made using a process which utilized an acid bath treatment. Each form was limited to a production of 1,000 pieces, which were signed by the glass artist. Glassworker Victor Hendryx is credited with developing the Guild Gossamer process. All items in this line are considered rare.

Iced

The Iced decoration was applied to Crystal jugs and tumblers, resulting in a frosty appearance, c. 1925. Amber, Blue, Green and Canary trim can be found on this ware.

Iridescent

Two iridescent colors were introduced in 1924, Yellow Iridescent and Regular Iridescent (Mother of Pearl). The Yellow Iridescent finish was achieved by a spray application to a Canary blank; the Mother of Pearl finish resulted from the spray application to a Crystal blank. This type of glassware was popular for a brief period of time.

Satin

Satin glass was produced by the United States Glass Company during the 1920s and 1930s and was very popular in tableware and decorative pieces as well. The satin finish was achieved by immersing the object in hydrofluoric acid. A limited amount of stemware was accented with a satin finish, including the "Draped Nude" stemline.

Stipple

A pressed tableware line, the Stipple decoration was introduced in 1924, and produced for only a brief period of time, primarily in jugs and tumblers. Known colors are Canary, Sky Blue, Amber, and Reflex Green.

Cascade

The Cascade line was introduced in 1938 and was designed by Robert A. Kelly for the United States Glass Company. A pressed Crystal pattern, Cascade was often highlighted with a partial satin finish. An extensive line, Cascade was produced in over 65 items.

"Flower Garden with Butterflies"

"Flower Garden with Butterflies" is a pressed design which was introduced in 1925. This line was originally known as line #15326, but is commonly known as "Flower Garden with Butterflies" by collectors today. Colors in this line are Crystal, Canary, Sky Blue, Amber, Reflex Green, Emerald Green and Rose Pink. These colors are sometimes highlighted with gold trim. The same pressed pattern was produced in Black and was named Brocade by the United States Glass Company. A catalog page described the pattern as "Bright Black Glass with Brocade Etching," page 136, *Tiffin Glassmasters, Book II,* by Fred Bickenheuser. The background of the Brocade pattern was etched to highlight the design. Although the patterns are identical, the items cataloged in the Brocade pattern are different shapes than those found in the #15326 line. The Brocade etching is also commonly referred to as "Flower Garden with Butterflies" by collectors today.

Octagon

Introduced in 1927, the Octagon line, #337, was produced in Rose Pink, Reflex Green, and Crystal in bright or satin finish. Twilite, Old Gold, and Black were added to the line in 1928. Octagon was produced at Factory K in Pittsburgh, Pennsylvania. The United States Glass Company insignia, an intertwined USG is often found embossed on the bottom of pieces in the Octagon line.

Velva

The Velva line, which is Art Deco in appearance, was introduced in 1937. Its distinctive feature is the satin finish, which was sometimes decorated with platinum. Known colors in the Velva line are Crystal Satin and Blue Satin. Tiffin also produced these shapes with a bright finish in Crystal, Blue, Topaz, and Black. The Velva line remains undocumented at this time.

Craquelle

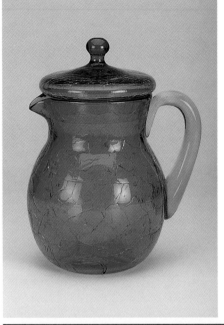

Blue with Canary trim #117, 64 oz. Covered Jug. $300-350

Crystal with Green trim #14194, 2 qt. Jug with cover; Crystal with Amber trim: #14185, Ice Tea; #14194, 2 qt. Jug with cover. $225-275, $20-30, $225-275

Canary #517, 12 oz. Tumbler; Canary with Blue trim #117, 64 oz. Covered Jug. $25-35, $300-350

Crystal with Green trim #117, 64 oz. Covered Jug, with cased glass finial. $200-250

This March 14, 1927, *China, Glass, and Lamps* advertisement features another style of tumbler and jug with the Craquelle finish.

China, Glass, and Lamps July 21, 1924.

Guild Gossamer

Crystal Guild Gossamer Tumbler. $45-65

Photograph of Victor Hendryx, who worked at Factory R from 1909-1938.

Fig.1.   *Fig.2.*

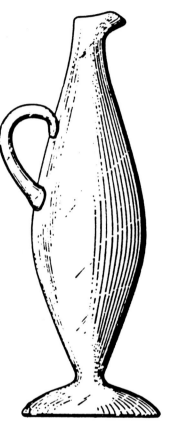

INVENTOR

Rowena Reed Kostellow

By *Thomas G. Miller*

Her attorney

Crystal 12 3/4 h. Handled Jug, signed Victor Hendryx, #177-8. $500-600   United States Patent Office drawing for Guild Gossamer items, filed February, 1938.

122

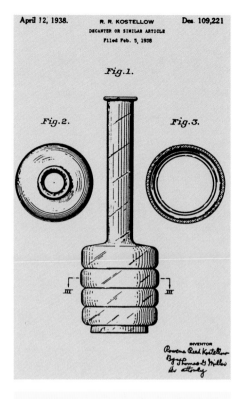

April 12, 1938.   R. R. KOSTELLOW   Des. 109,221
DECANTER OR SIMILAR ARTICLE
Filed Feb. 5, 1938

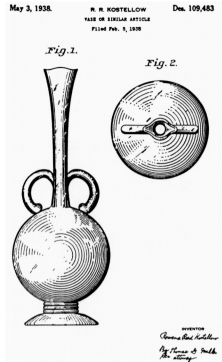

May 3, 1938.   R. R. KOSTELLOW   Des. 109,483
VASE OR SIMILAR ARTICLE
Filed Feb. 5, 1938

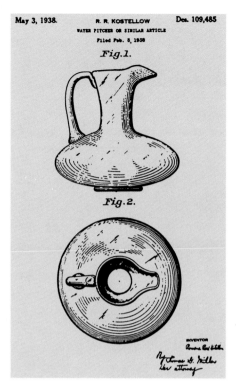

May 3, 1938.   R. R. KOSTELLOW   Des. 109,485
WATER PITCHER OR SIMILAR ARTICLE
Filed Feb. 5, 1938

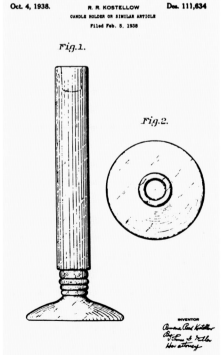

Oct. 4, 1938.   R. R. KOSTELLOW   Des. 111,634
CANDLE HOLDER OR SIMILAR ARTICLE
Filed Feb. 5, 1938

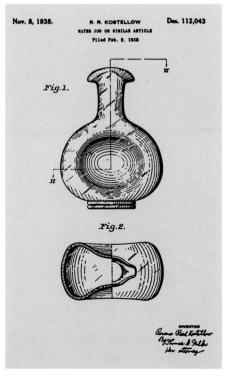

Nov. 8, 1938.   R. R. KOSTELLOW   Des. 112,043
WATER JUG OR SIMILAR ARTICLE
Filed Feb. 5, 1938

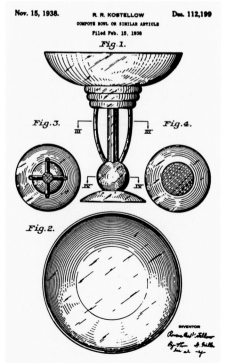

Nov. 15, 1938.   R. R. KOSTELLOW   Des. 112,199
COMPOTE BOWL OR SIMILAR ARTICLE
Filed Feb. 15, 1938

United States Patent Office drawings
for Guild Gossamer items, filed
February, 1938.

Iced

Crystal with Blue trim: #14194, 2 qt. Jug with cover; #14185, Ice Tea. Crystal with Amber trim: #14185, Ice Tea; #14194, 2 qt. Jug with cover. $250-300, $20-30, $20-30, $200-250

Crystal: #580, 10 oz. Table Tumblers; #117 Covered Jug. $15-25 each, $150-200

Crystal: #354, Handled Tumblers; #127, 2 qt. Tall Covered Jug. $20-30 each, $150-200

Crystal with Amber trim #112, 72 oz. Jug. $150-200

Iridescent

Yellow Iridescent #14180, 9 oz. Goblet, Wide Optic. $20-30

Regular Iridescent (Mother of Pearl) with Rose Pink trim #15001, Goblets, Wide Optic. $20-30 each

In addition to these illustrations, the following items are also listed:
No. 14180, 2½ oz. Wine, No. 354, 5 oz. Tumbler.

No 14180. 9 oz.
Goblet.

No. 14180
Cafe Parfait.

No. 14180
Saucer Champagne.

No. 14180. 3½ oz.
Cocktail.

No. 14180
Oyster Cocktail or Egg.

No. 14180
Sundae.

No. 9268
Marmalade and Cover.

No. 354
12 oz. Tumbler.
Also furnish with Handle and
14 oz. No Handle.

No. 354
10 oz. Ale Tumbler.

No. 354
10 oz. Table.

No. 1080/8814
Finger Bowl and Plate.

No. 14185
10 in. Bud Vase.

No. 13630.   Jug, 2 Quart.

Plate 765-Yellow.

United States Glass Company catalog page featuring the #14180 line with Yellow Iridescent finish.

Satin

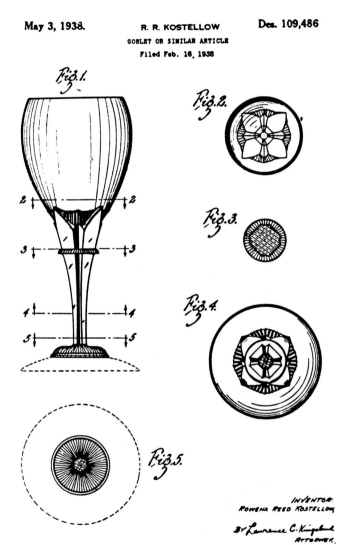

May 3, 1938.   R. R. KOSTELLOW   Des. 109,486
GOBLET OR SIMILAR ARTICLE
Filed Feb. 16, 1938

Fig.1.

Fig.2.

Fig.3.

Fig.4.

Fig.5.

INVENTOR:
ROWENA REED KOSTELLOW

BY Lawrence C. Kingsland
ATTORNEY.

United States Patent Office drawing for #17306 stemline, filed February 16, 1938.

Crystal #17306-1, Goblet, Cocktail, Saucer Champagne, satin finish stem. The #17306 stemline has a bright finish. The #17306 stemline was designed by Rowena Reed Kostellow. $30-40, $25-35, $25-35

127

Crystal Satin: #444, 12 oz. Tumblers; #6461, 2 qt. Ice Tea Jug with cover. $20-30 each, $275-325

Sky Blue Satin #6455, 2 qt. Covered Jug, Silver Overlay. $300-350

China, Glass, and Lamps, June 8, 1925.

Stipple

Sky Blue #6461, 2 qt.
Ice Tea Jug and
cover. $175-225

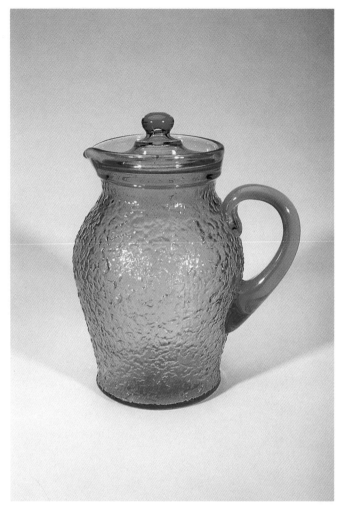

Amber with Jasper trim
#6461, 2 qt. Ice Tea
Jug. $150-200

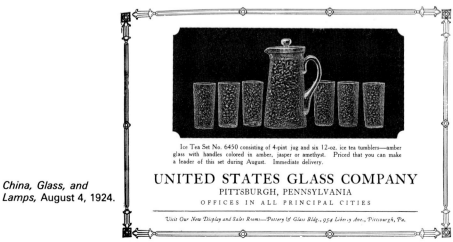

Ice Tea Set No. 6450 consisting of 4-pint jug and six 12-oz. ice tea tumblers—amber glass with handles colored in amber, jasper or amethyst. Priced that you can make a leader of this set during August. Immediate delivery.

UNITED STATES GLASS COMPANY
PITTSBURGH, PENNSYLVANIA
OFFICES IN ALL PRINCIPAL CITIES

Visit Our New Display and Sales Rooms—Pottery & Glass Bldg., 954 Liberty Ave., Pittsburgh, Pa.

China, Glass, and Lamps, August 4, 1924.

Stippled Ice Tea Set

A low priced ice tea set in the new stippled glass effect. Order by No. 6461, 4 pint jug and 12 oz. Fancy Shape Ice Tea, Stippled. Packs 12 sets per barrel. Also supplied No. 6450 straight shape jug and ice teas at same prices.

UNITED STATES GLASS COMPANY
PITTSBURGH, PENNSYLVANIA
OFFICES IN ALL PRINCIPAL CITIES

Visit Our New Display and Sales Rooms—Pottery & Glass Bldg., 954 Liberty Ave., Pittsburgh, Pa.

China, Glass, and Lamps, July 28, 1924.

Cascade

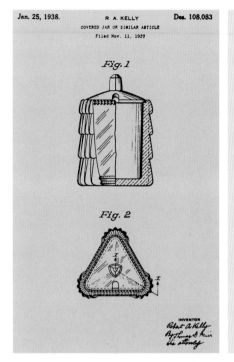

Jan. 25, 1938. R. A. KELLY Des. 108,083
COVERED JAR OR SIMILAR ARTICLE
Filed Nov. 11, 1937

Fig. 1

Fig. 2

INVENTOR
Robert A. Kelly
By Thomas G. Kerr
his attorney

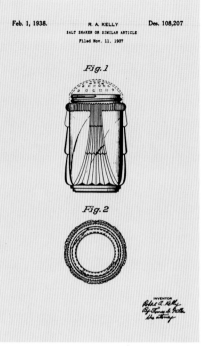

Feb. 1, 1938. R. A. KELLY Des. 108,207
SALT SHAKER OR SIMILAR ARTICLE
Filed Nov. 11, 1937

Fig. 1

Fig. 2

INVENTOR
Robert A. Kelly
By Thomas G. Miller
his attorney

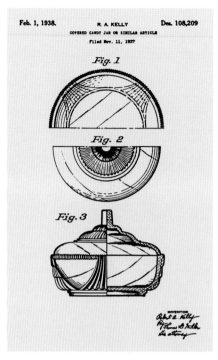

Feb. 1, 1938. R. A. KELLY Des. 108,209
COVERED CANDY JAR OR SIMILAR ARTICLE
Filed Nov. 11, 1937

Fig. 1

Fig. 2

Fig. 3

INVENTOR
Robert A. Kelly
By Thomas G. Miller
his attorney

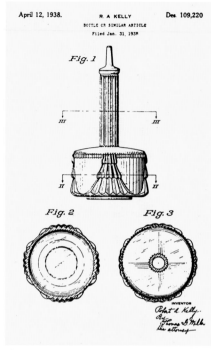

April 12, 1938. R. A. KELLY Des. 109,220
BOTTLE OR SIMILAR ARTICLE
Filed Jan. 31, 1938

Fig. 1

Fig. 2 Fig. 3

INVENTOR
Robert A. Kelly
By Thomas G. Miller
his attorney

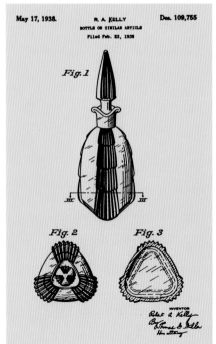

May 17, 1938. R. A. KELLY Des. 109,755
BOTTLE OR SIMILAR ARTICLE
Filed Feb. 23, 1938

Fig. 1

Fig. 2 Fig. 3

INVENTOR
Robert A. Kelly
By Thomas G. Miller
His attorney

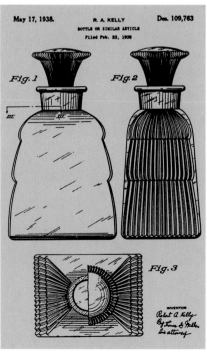

May 17, 1938. R. A. KELLY Des. 109,763
BOTTLE OR SIMILAR ARTICLE
Filed Feb. 23, 1938

Fig. 1 Fig. 2

Fig. 3

INVENTOR
Robert A. Kelly
By Thomas G. Miller
his attorney

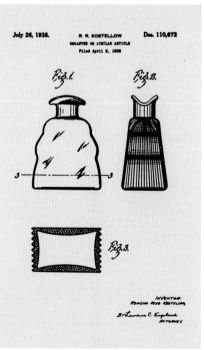

July 26, 1938. R. R. KOSTELLOW Des. 110,672
DECANTER OR SIMILAR ARTICLE
Filed April 8, 1938

Fig. 1 Fig. 2

Fig. 3

INVENTOR
ROWENA REED KOSTELLOW
BY Laurence C. Kingsland
ATTORNEY

United States Patent Office drawings for Cascade items, filed from November 11, 1937 to April 8, 1938.

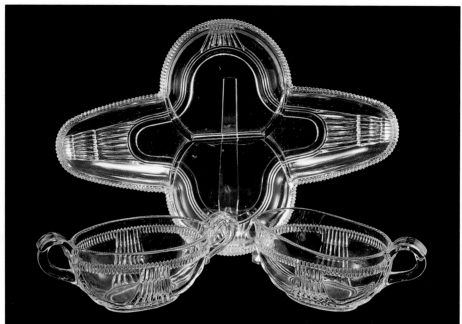

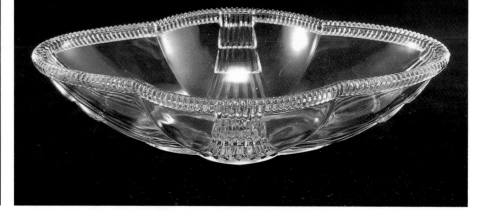

Top: Crystal #15365, 9" Salad Bowl. $40-60

Bottom: Crystal #15365, 9" Cookie Jar and cover. $100-125

Top: Crystal: #15365, 12" 4-Part Relish Tray; #15365, Cream and Sugar. $40-60, $50-75 set

Bottom: Crystal #15365, 14" Oval Centerpiece Bowl. $40-60

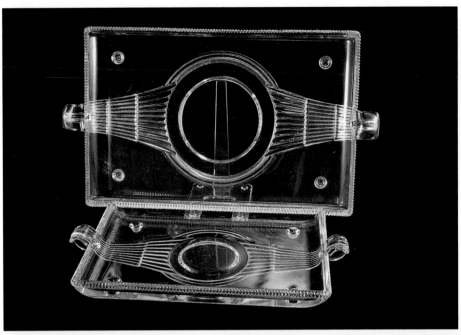

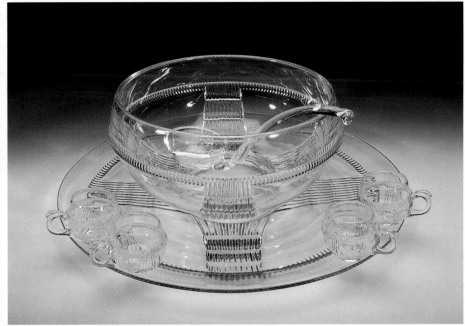

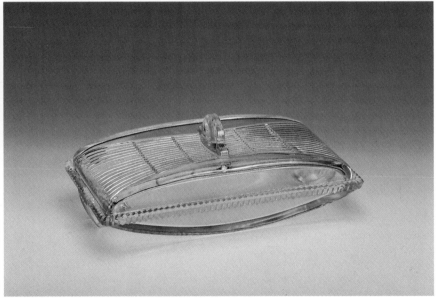

Top left: Crystal: #15365, 14 3/4" Large Hostess Tray; #15365, 11 1/2" Small Hostess Tray. $45-65 each

Top right: Crystal #15365, 12 1/2" Punch Bowl, 20" Plate; Punch Cups. $100-125, $65-85, $10-15 each

Bottom left: Crystal #15365, 10" h. Vase. $50-75

Bottom center: Crystal #15365, 4 1/4" h. Oil or Vinegar Bottle; 6 1/2" h. Compote. 30-50 each

Bottom right: Crystal #15365, 8 1/2" Covered Cigarette Box. $45-70

Crystal #15365, 9" 2-Lite Candelabra. $100-125 pair

Bottom left: Crystal #15365, 6 3/4" Diamond Ash Tray, 5" Oblong Ash Trays, 2 3/4" Triangular Ash Trays. The diamond and triangular ash trays were originally sold as a 3-piece Diamond Ash Tray set. $15-25, $20-30 each, $15-25 each

Bottom center: Crystal #15365, 10 oz. Goblet. $15-25

Crystal: #15365, 4 oz. Claret; #17322, 10 oz. Goblet; #15365, 2 1/2 oz. Cocktail. Note the different line numbers for the similar stems. $10-20, $15-25, $10-20

#15361 Line

"Flower Garden with Butterflies"

#15361 Line catalog page

United States Glass Company, Pittsburgh, Pa., U. S. A.
15361 Line

15361. 5½ in. Nappy
2 Handled

15361. 9½ in. Bowl
Nouvelle

15361. Candleholder
1-Lite

5831. Candelabrum
2-Lite

15361. 11¼ in. Centerpiece

15361. 6 in. Comport
Tall

15361. Creme Soup
and Plate

15361. Cup and Saucer

15361. Mayonnaise Set
with Ladle

15361. 7½ in. Pickle Tray
also
15361. 10¼ in. Celery Tray

15361. 6 in. Plate
2 Handled

15361. Plate
6 in., 7½ in. and 9½ in. Sizes

15361. 10¼ in. Cake Plate
2 Handled

15361. Sugar and Cream

15361. 6 in. Bon Bon Tray

Printed in U.S.A.

500-2-36

Plate 220

This February 1936 United States Glass Company catalog page identifies the #15361 line.
These blanks were sometimes decorated with plate etched patterns.

Reflex Green #15326, 10 1/2" h. Vase. $225-275

134

Top: Amber, Sky Blue, Rose Pink #15326, 6 1/4" Whipped Creams and Ladles. $70-90, $75-100, $75-100

Bottom: Rose Pink #15326, 7 1/2" h. Comport; Amber #15326, 6" h. Puff Box with gold decoration. $120-160, $95-115

Top: Emerald Green #15326, Console Set: 8 1/2" Candlesticks, 10" Low Footed Comport. $150-200 pair, $100-150

Bottom: Canary #15326, 8" Plate with Gold trim; Rose Pink #15326, 6" Sugar; Emerald Green #15326, 8" Plate. $35-45, $50-70, $20-25

Top left: Emerald Green #15326, 6" h. Puff Box with gold decoration; 7 1/2" h. Comport. $120-160 each

Top right: Detail of ""Flower Garden with Butterflies."

Bottom left: Canary #15326, 7 1/2" h. Conic Candy Jar; Amber #15326, 6" Combination Smoker's Tray. $125-165, $125-150

Bottom right: *China, Glass, and Lamps,* August 3, 1925, advertisement showing the #15326 "Flower Garden with Butterflies" Covered Comport.

United States Glass Company, Pittsburgh, Pa., U. S. A.
No. 326. PATTERN ROSE PINK. TRANSPARENT,
Also furnished in Blue and Light Green. Transparent.

Factory K
200-11-26-26

No. 326-10 inch Hld. Cake Plate.
Price per Dozen,
Rose Pink, $23.00
Blue or Green, 21.00

No. 326-Cologne and Stopper.
Price per Dozen,
Rose Pink, $20.00
Blue or Green, 18.00

No. 326-5 inch Comport and Cover.
Price per Dozen,
Rose Pink, $14.00
Blue or Green, 12.80

No. 326-10 inch Low Ft. Comport, Fld.
Price per Dozen,
Rose Pink, $23.00
Blue or Green, 21.00

No. 326. Whipped Cream and Ladle.
Price per Dozen,
Rose Pink, $17.60
Blue or Green, 16.00

No. 326-Low Ft. Puff Box and Cover.
Price per Dozen,
Rose Pink, $13.80
Blue or Green, 12.60

No. 326-Cheese and Cracker Set.
Price per Dozen,
Rose Pink, $22.50
Blue or Green, 20.50

*No. 326-8 inch Hi. Ft. Comport.
*Price per Doz. Rose Pink, $20.00, Blue or Green, $18.00

No. 326-Roll Tray.
Price per Dozen,
Rose Pink, $20.50
Blue or Green, 18.50

No. 326-Conic Candy Jar and Cover.
Price per Dozen,
Rose Pink, $17.60
Blue or Green, 16.00

No. 326-8 inch Plate.
Price per Dozen,
Rose Pink, $9.60
Blue or Green, 8.70

No. 326-10½ inch Vase.
Price per Dozen,
Rose Pink, $31.00
Blue or Green, 28.00

(In addition to the items shown the following items are also listed,
Candlestick--7 inch and 10 inch Hi. Ft. Comports--7 inch and 10 inch Plates--
6 inch Ftd. Vase--Candy Box and Cover and Ash Tray.)

THE MERIDEN GRAVURE CO.

296

United States Glass Company catalog page featuring the #15326 line, "Flower Garden with Butterflies."

Black: #15319, 10" h. 2-handled Vase;
#15320, 9" h. Wall Vase. $250-300 each

Black #15179, 7" Covered
Naturtium Bowl and base.
$250-300

138

Black: #15179, 8"
Cupped Comport;
#79, 6" h. Candle-
sticks. $200-250,
$250-300 pair

Black #15320, 10"
Footed Cheese
and Cracker set.
$300-350 set

UNITED STATES GLASS CO., PITTSBURGH, PA., U. S. A.

No. 337—OCTAGON SERVICE PATTERN.

Furnished in Green and Pink colors.   In Bright or Satin Finish.

Factory K

225-3-14-27

No. 337-Salad and Cover, Oblong Shape.

No. 337-Boullion Cup.

No, 337-Cup and Saucer.

No. 337-Cheese and Cracker Set.

No. 337-Cake Plate, Hld.

No. 337-Soup Bowl.

No. 337-Sugar.

No. 337-Cream.

15-Piece Bridge Set, Consists of,
½ Doz-Cups and Saucers   ⅟₁₂ Doz-Sugar and Cream Set.
½ Doz-Salad Plates 8 in.   ⅟₁₂ Doz-Cake Plate Hld.

27-Piece Service Set, Consists of,
½ Doz-Cups   ½ Doz-B & B Plates 6 in.
½ Doz-Saucers   ⅟₁₂ Doz-Sugar and Cream Set.
½ Doz-Salad Plates   ⅟₁₂ Doz-Cake Plate Hld.

No. 337-10 inch Service Plate.

No. 337-Salad Plate

No. 337-B & B Plate.

No. 1   No. 2   No. 337-S & P Shakers.

No. 337—9 in. Comport.

300

No. Item	Bright-Satin	No. Item	Bright-Satin	No. Item	Bright-Satin	No. Item	Bright-Satin
No. 337-Sugar,	$8.00 $10.00	No. 337-Soup Bowl,	$12.00 $15.00	337-S & P Shaker No. 1	$6.40 $8.00	337-Service Plate, 10″	$16.00 $20.00
No. 337-Cream,	8.00 10.00	No. 337-Boullion Cup,	8.00 10.00	337-S & P Shaker No. No. 2,	5.30 6.60	337-Salad & Cover	32.00 40.00
No. 337-Cup,	5.20 6.50	No. 337-Comport 9 in.,	26.50 33.00	337-B & P Plate, 6″	5 20 6 50	337-Bridge Set, (15-Pce).	101.60 129.50
No. 337-Saucer,	5.20 6.50	No. 337-Cake Plate Hld.	13.20 16.50	337-Salad Plate, 8″	8.00 10.00	337-Service Set, (27-Pce)	169.60 212.00

No. 337—Cheese and Cracker Set, Bright, $18.70—Satin, $23.30

THE MERIDEN GRAVURE CO.

United States Glass Company December 13, 1928, catalog page for #337 Octagon line.

140

Announcing
The smart new **OCTAGON** *bridge set*

For women who know how to entertain

HOSTESSES quickly recognize the charm and smartness that will be added to their Bridge parties and luncheons by this new and distinguished-looking Bridge-luncheon set.

It is fashioned in the latest and much-wanted Octagonal design . . of finer hand-finished, fire-polished pot glass. Ready for shipment now—in both *rose-pink* and the new *apple-green* glass.

Ask for No. 337 Bridge set—4 eight-inch salad plates; 4 cups; 4 saucers; 1 cake plate (handled); 1 sugar and cream set; and 4 iced teas (blown). Sold with or without iced teas—15 pieces or 19 pieces.

A bridge-luncheon table, neatly set with No. 337 and PROMINENTLY DISPLAYED IN YOUR WINDOW will increase sales—especially in hot weather.

Your customers recognize the U. S. G. Co. shield as the guarantee of finer quality in household glassware.

Ask our salesman about the new No. 337—27 piece complete service set—rose-pink and apple-green.

UNITED STATES GLASS COMPANY
World's Largest Makers of Household Glassware.
PITTSBURGH, PA.
Sales Offices in All Principal Cities.

The Octagon #337 line was introduced in this 1927 *China, Glass, and Lamps* advertisement.

Blue 6" h. Candleholders, satin finish. $125-150 pair

Crystal: Sugar and Cream; 10 1/2" h. Vase, satin finish. $60-85 set, $100-125

Top: Crystal: 11" Oval Bowl, 15" Oval Liner Plate. Both satin finish. $85-115, $65-95

Bottom: Blue: 10 1/2" h. Vase; 12" Flared Bowl, satin finish. $125-150, $75-100

Top: Blue: Mayonnaise and Underplate; 6" 2-handled Bowl with cover, satin finish. $50-75 set, $100-125

Bottom: Crystal 7 3/4" 2-handled Bowl, satin finish. $45-65

Company Photos.

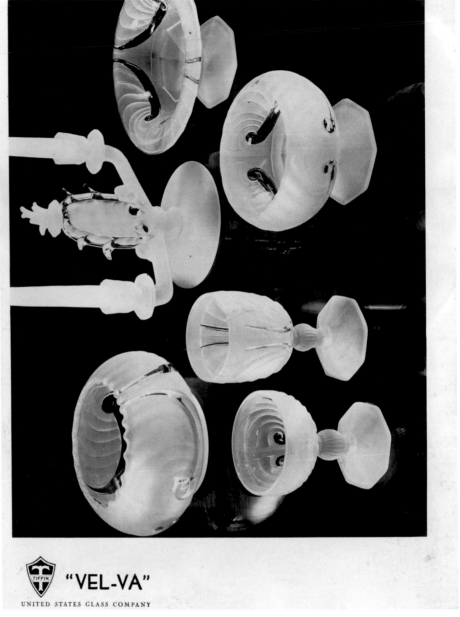

144

Chapter 7: Colored Ware

Color is one of the most outstanding features of the tableware produced at Factory R. Many of the items included in this chapter are examples of undecorated ware that have remained favorites of consumers from the 1920s to the present time.

March 1924, *The Glass Outlook*, a United States Glass Company publication.

Blown Stemware in the Making

THE first thing that comes to the mind of the average buyer of blown stemware is, "Why does it cost so much?" After a tour of inspection in a plant where stemware is made, the wonder is that it can be sold so cheaply.

The first three steps in the development of a piece of blown stemware are practically the same as in the making of pressed ware, discussed in the February Glass Outlook. First, a sketch is made, then a plaster model and then a mould is made of chilled iron. From this step on the operations, however, are quite different. The glass-blower stands on a platform just outside an opening leading into the furnace containing the molten glass. He dips the end of a long iron pipe into the glass, withdraws it from the furnace and blows until the glass has assumed the shape of a small cylinder. Another workman now takes the pipe, opens the mould at his feet which is in two parts, hinged together, and with the pipe held in a vertical position he inserts the small glass cylinder in the mould, closes it by means of a foot lever, and continues to blow with the glass held inside the mould. The mould is opened, the glass removed and it is then turned over to two other men, one of whom draws a small gob of molten glass from the furnace and sticks it to the end of the elonga-

Blowing a Goblet

Putting Foot on Goblet

Cutting Off Top of Goblet

Grinding Top of Goblet Smooth

tion of the blown glass, thus forming the base or foot. The piece of stemware, if it is a champagne glass, has now assumed the shape shown in the left hand illustration at the bottom of this page. It is now passed through the lehr for tempering and when it emerges it passes to the machine which cuts off the upper part, giving the glass its finished shape, shown below. The next step is to grind down the edges where the top has just been removed. This is done by means of a rapidly revolving abrasive wheel and another machine through which it goes for its last operation, called the glazing machine. Here an extremely hot flame is played on the ground edge at the top, giving it a smooth finished edge.

Goblet with Foot as it passes thru Lehr.

A Finished Piece of Stemware

188. Goblet

188. Sau. Champ.

188. Sundae

921. Cafe Parfait

188. Claret

188. Wine

188. Cocktail

Note:- For complete itemization of this line,
see other side.

Printed in U.S.A.

630. Oyster
Cocktail

196/8814. Finger Bowl and Plate

251/881. Grape Fruit and Liner

185. Table

194. Jug and Cover

Plate 765-188 Rambler Rose.

United States Glass Company catalog page featuring the Rambler Rose gold band, c. 1920s.

146

001-8 oz. Goblet
$8.25

001-6 oz. Sau. Champ.
$8.25

001. Sundae
$7.80

001. Cafe Parfait
$8.25

001-2 oz. Wine
$7.50

001-3 oz. Cocktail
$7.50

001-1 oz. Cordial
$7.25

630. Oyster
Cocktail, $7.80

Note: In addition to items illustrated, the following are also listed: 8814-6 inch Plate (Not Optic, All Rose) $8.70;
8833-8 inch Plate (Not Optic, All Rose) $12.90; 020-2
oz. Ftd. Whiskey, $8.25; 020-10 oz. Ftd. Table, $9.00

185—Ftd. Finger
Bowl $13.50

020—5 oz. Ftd.
Seltzer, $8.50

020—12 oz. Ftd.
Ice Tea, $10.00

9712—2 Qt. Ftd. Jug and
Cover, $57.00
Also furnish without
Cover, $45.00

No. 6 Sugar
$18.00

No. 6 Cream
$15.00

251—Grape Fruit, $27.00
Also furnish 881 Liner
(Crystal, Not Optic) $6.00

Plate 365—001 Rose-Green.

United States Glass Company catalog page illustrating the #15001 line in Rose with Green trim and Festoon Optic, c.
late 1920s.

147

DISTINCTIVE DESIGNS

feature the lead-blown stemware of which three Goblets are shown. Optic bowls of graceful shapes, with knobbed, fluted and bulbous stems (some with green, amber and other colored trim) offer variety which attracts the hostess seeking something new for her table and pleases her guests in the perfection of her service. Goblets, Footed Table and Seltzer Tumblers and Ice Tea Glasses are some of the items in these lines, full details of which can be secured from the home office or our various sales agencies, which are conveniently located in all large cities.

UNITED STATES GLASS COMPANY

PITTSBURGH, PA.

No. 011 TABLEWARE LINE

(PATENT APPLIED FOR)

Plain in its simplicity and simple in its plainness, but so graceful that the buyer responds instantly to its appeal.

Scintillating lead glass, with Optic crystal bowls, and green, amber or lilac trim.

The line has been developed for a complete table service, and includes Goblets, Tumblers and Jugs; Finger Bowls and Plates; Sugar and Cream Sets; Sundaes; Saucer Champagnes; Wines; Cocktails; Cafe Parfaits; etc., etc.

UNITED STATES GLASS COMPANY

PITTSBURGH, PENNSYLVANIA.

There are samples at our Sales Offices, and we have color plates showing the principal items.

Top left: *China, Glass, and Lamps*, 1926.

Top right: *China, Glass, and Lamps*, August 8, 1926.

NUMBER 017

PATENT APPLIED FOR

THE BEE HIVE LINE

ROSE-PINK
CRYSTAL—With GREEN OR AMBER TRIM

A design unique in its contour and finish, which appeals to the discriminating buyer who wants something striking and novel.

There are narrow encircling flutes on the bodies and the stems, and the same motif is repeated on the knob of the jug. This detail, in combination with the full wide optic, brings out charming high lights in the brilliant lead-blown ware.

"A Complete Service"

UNITED STATES GLASS COMPANY

PITTSBURGH, PA.

Sales Offices in all Principal Cities

China, Glass, and Lamps, December 13, 1926.

Reflex Green #14188 Goblet, Wide
Optic, Valencia gold band. $25-35

Left group: Crystal with Nile Green trim, Saucer Champagne, Goblet. Both
Wide Optic, unknown line number. This goblet is an unusual 10" tall, com-
pared with the average 7-8" goblet. $25-35, $30-40.
Right group: Crystal with Reflex Green trim #15015, Saucer Champagne,
Goblet, Cordial. All Spiral Optic. $10-20, $15-25, $25-35

Crystal with Reflex Green trim #15022, Saucer
Champagne, Goblet, Wine. All Spiral Optic.
Designed by Virgil Loomis. The "button" in the
stem is cased glass. $30-40, $35-45, $30-40

Crystal with Blue trim #15015, Goblet, Saucer Champagne, Cordial, Grapefruit. All Spiral Optic. $20-30, $15-25, $40-50, $25-35

Crystal with Green trim #15038, Saucer Champagne, Wide Optic. $15-25

Crystal with Amber trim #15002, Ice Tea, Wine, Goblet, Saucer Champagne. All Wide Optic. The stem on the ice tea is hand formed, while the others are pressed. $15-25, $15-25, $20-30, $15-25.

Crystal with Nile Green trim #15003, Goblet with cased "button;" Crystal with Amber trim #15001, Goblet. Both with Herringbone Optic. $35-45, $25-35.

Green: #15028, Saucer Champagne, Sundae, Goblet, Cordial; #112, 2 qt. Squat Jug. All Diamond Optic. $10-20, $10-20, $15-25, $20-30, $50-75

Crystal with Royal Blue trim #15079, 5 oz. Champagne, 9 oz. Goblets. The champagne is not the traditional saucer champagne shape. $50-75 each

Amber #15040, Goblets, Wide Optic, Laurel gold band. $25-35 each

Crystal with Amber trim #15064, Goblet, Festoon Optic,
Saucer Champagne, Wide Optic, Byzantine etching; Crystal
with Black trim #15064, Saucer Champagne, Wide Optic;
Mandarin with Crystal trim #15064, Wine, Festoon Optic. $10-
20, $10-20, $10-15, $10-15

Crystal with Reflex Green trim #15064, 9 1/2"
h. Bud Vases, Wide Optic. $55-75 each

Rose Pink with Reflex Green trim #15024, Goblet, Festoon Optic. $35-45

Rose Pink with Reflex Green trim: #6, Cream and Sugar; #9712, 2 qt. Jug; #15024, Wine, Goblet, Saucer Champagne, Cordial; #14185, Ice Tea; #15024, Sundae. All Festoon Optic. $100-125 set, $275-325, $30-40, $35-45, $30-40, $75-100, $30-40, $30-40.

Top left: Crystal with Blue trim #15001, Goblet, Wide Optic. $20-30

Top center: Crystal with Blue trim #15002, Goblet, Saucer Champagne. Both Spiral Optic. $20-30, $15-25

Top right: Crystal with Canary trim #15024, Goblet, Wide Optic. $20-30

Bottom left: Mandarin with Crystal trim #15067, Saucer Champagne, Wide Optic. $20-30

Bottom center: Crystal with Nile Green trim #15001, Goblet, unidentified optic. $20-30

Bottom right: Rose Pink with Reflex Green trim #112, Squat Jug, unidentified optic. $175-225

154

Top left: Lilac with Crystal trim #6, Sugar and Cream, Wide Optic. $75-100 set

Top right: Canary #4, Sugar and Cream, Wide Optic. $75-100 set

Bottom right: Royal Blue with Crystal trim #15076, Saucer Champagne; Crystal with Amber trim #15076, 10" h. Bud Vase. Both Wide Optic. $30-40, $40-65

No. 14196. 9 oz.
Goblet.
Blue Foot.

No. 14196.
Saucer Champagne.
Blue Foot.

No. 14196. 2 oz.
Wine.
Blue Foot.

No. 14196. 2½ oz.
Cocktail.
Blue Foot.

No. 14196.
Sundae.
Blue Foot.

No. 9705. 7 in.
Hi. Comport.
Blue Foot.

No. 14185. 10 in.
Bud Vase.
Blue Foot.

No. 14185. 12 oz.
Tumbler.
Blue Foot.

No. 14185. 8½ oz.
Table.
Blue Foot.

No. 354. 14 oz.
Hdl. Tumbler.
Blue Handle.
Also furnished without Handle.

No. 354. 10 oz.
Table.

No. 9701
Candy Box and Cover.
Blue Knob on Cover.

No. 127
Tall Covered Jug, 2 Qt.
Blue Knob on Cover.
Blue Handle.

No. 14194
Foot and Covered Jug, 2 Qt.
Blue Foot, Handle and Cover.
Also furnished without Cover.

Plate 365-Canary.

United States Glass Company catalog page featuring Canary with Blue trim, c. 1924.

156

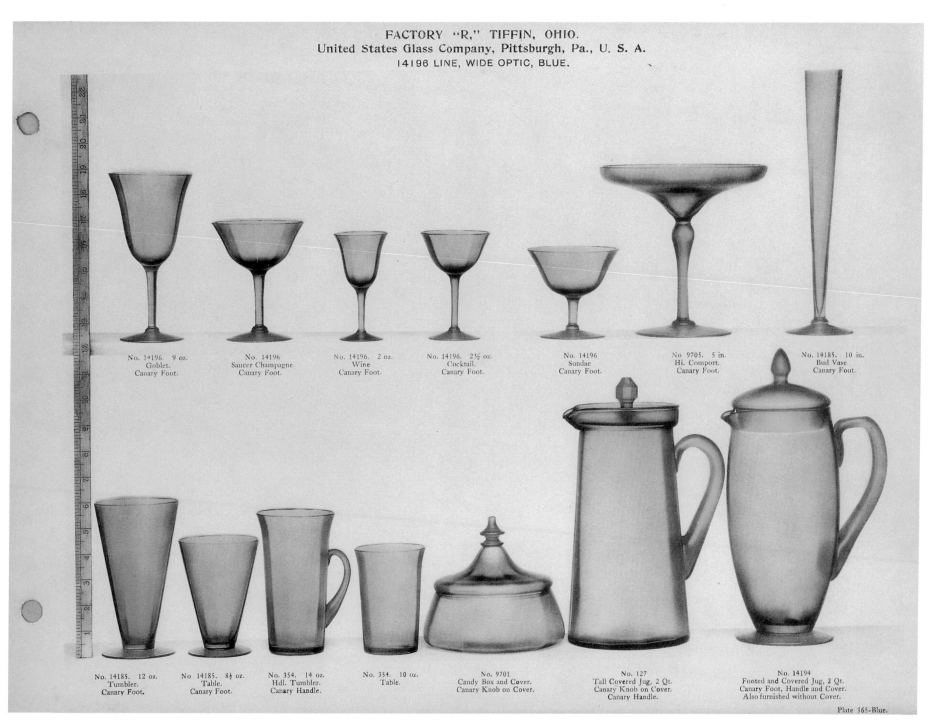

No. 14196. 9 oz.
Goblet.
Canary Foot.

No. 14196.
Saucer Champagne.
Canary Foot.

No. 14196. 2 oz.
Wine
Canary Foot.

No. 14196. 2½ oz.
Cocktail.
Canary Foot.

No. 14196
Sundae
Canary Foot.

No 9705. 5 in.
Hi. Comport.
Canary Foot.

No. 14185. 10 in.
Bud Vase
Canary Foot.

No. 14185. 12 oz.
Tumbler.
Canary Foot.

No 14185. 8½ oz.
Table.
Canary Foot.

No. 354. 14 oz.
Hdl. Tumbler.
Canary Handle.

No. 354. 10 oz.
Table.

No. 9701
Candy Box and Cover.
Canary Knob on Cover.

No. 127
Tall Covered Jug, 2 Qt.
Canary Knob on Cover.
Canary Handle.

No. 14194
Footed and Covered Jug, 2 Qt.
Canary Foot, Handle and Cover.
Also furnished without Cover.

Plate 365-Blue.

United States Glass Company catalog page featuring Blue with Canary trim, c. 1924.

157

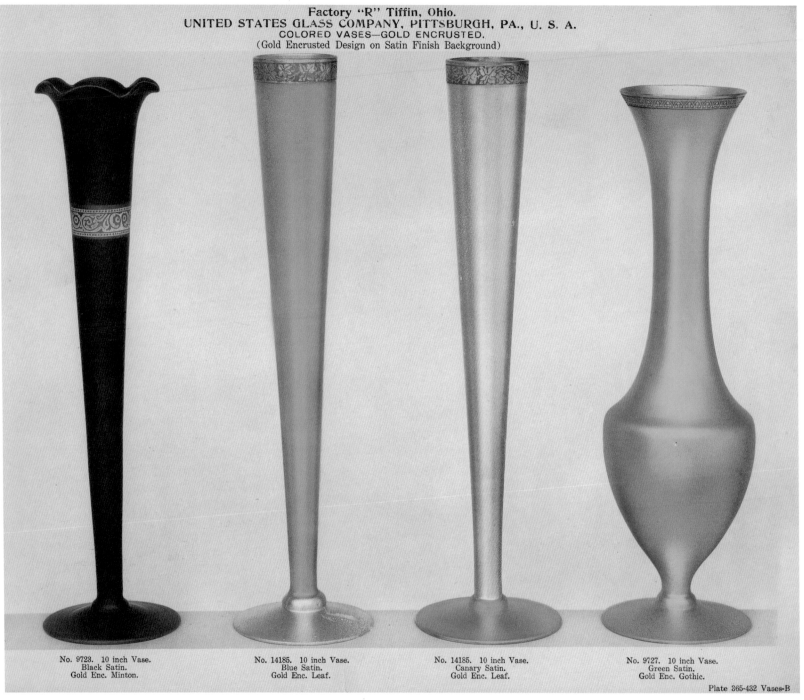

Factory "R" Tiffin, Ohio.
UNITED STATES GLASS COMPANY, PITTSBURGH, PA., U. S. A.
COLORED VASES—GOLD ENCRUSTED.
(Gold Encrusted Design on Satin Finish Background)

No. 9723. 10 inch Vase.
Black Satin.
Gold Enc. Minton.

No. 14185. 10 inch Vase.
Blue Satin.
Gold Enc. Leaf.

No. 14185. 10 inch Vase.
Canary Satin.
Gold Enc. Leaf.

No. 9727. 10 inch Vase.
Green Satin.
Gold Enc. Gothic.

Plate 365-432 Vases-B

United States Glass
Company catalog
page featuring
various bud vases.
The Gothic gold band
is documented here
for the first time. The
Blue and Canary color
combination on the
#14185 bud vase was
discontinued in 1929.

Blue with Canary trim, Wide Optic: #14196, Sundae, Wine, Goblet, Cocktail, Saucer Champagne; #14185, Seltzer, Ice Tea, Table Tumbler; #354, Handled Tumbler. $20-30, $20-30, $25-35, $20-30, $20-30, $20-30, $20-30, $20-30, $30-40

Top: Blue with Canary trim #15001, Cocktail, Goblet; Canary with Blue trim #15001, Saucer Champagne, Goblet, Cocktail. All Wide Optic. $25-35, $30-40, $25-35, $30-40, $25-35
Bottom: Canary with Blue trim #114, 3 pt. Jug; Blue with Canary trim #114, 3 pt. Jug. Both Wide Optic. $225-275 each

Top: Blue with Canary trim #9557, ½ lb. Candy Jar; Canary with Blue trim #14196, Wine, Saucer Champagne, Goblet, Cocktail. All Wide Optic. $125-150, $20-30, $20-30, $25-35, $20-30
Bottom: Canary with Blue trim #9705, 7" h. Comport, Wide Optic; Blue with Canary trim #14185, 7 1/4" h. Crimped Bud Vase; Canary with Blue trim: #14185, 10 1/4" Bud Vase; #14185, 7 1/4" Crimped Bud Vase; Blue with Canary trim #115, 2 qt. Jug and cover, Wide Optic. $125-150, $55-75, $55-75, $55-75, $250-300

Blue with Canary stem, 11 3/4" h. Vase; Blue with Canary trim, 11" h. Vase. Both Wide Optic. Attributed to Tiffin Glass. $200-250 each

Canary with Blue trim, 9 1/2" h. blown Candlesticks; Blue with Canary and Amber stem, 9 1/2" h. Compote. Both items Wide Optic. Attributed to Tiffin Glass. $225-275 pair, $225-275

Blue with Canary trim, Canary with Blue trim #14194, 2 qt. Jugs with covers, Wide Optic. $300-350 each

Canary with Blue trim #115, 62 oz. Covered Ice Tea Jug, Wide Optic, sterling silver "Clipper Ship" decoration. $300-350

Chapter 8: "Draped Nudes"

The #15078 stemline was produced c. 1934 for a brief period of time in nine shapes. Royal Blue, Crystal and Reflex Green, in bright or satin finish, were colors offered in this line. Stemware only was produced, some with optic. This stemline is commonly referred to as "Draped Nudes" by collectors today.

Crystal #15078, 4 oz. Claret; 9 oz Goblet; 1 1/4 oz. Large Cordial; 5 1/2 oz. Saucer Champagne; 1 1/4 oz. Large Cordial. Bright or satin finish stems. $150-200, $125-175, $175-225, $150-200, $175-225

Detail of #15078 stem.

Detail of #15078 stem.

Crystal with Royal Blue trim #15078, Goblet, Wine, Cocktail, Cordial, Saucer Champagne, with bright or satin finish. The wine goblet has Wide Optic and a Royal Blue foot. $225-275, $225-275, $225-275, $250-300, $225-275

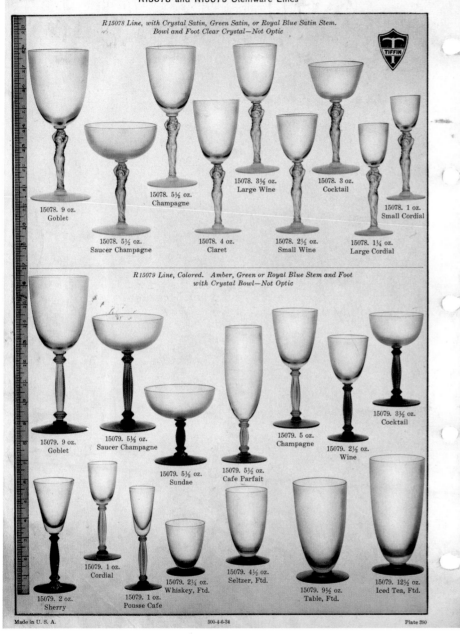

United States Glass Company, Pittsburgh, Pa., U.S.A.

R15078 and R15079 Stemware Lines

R 15078 Line, with Crystal Satin, Green Satin, or Royal Blue Satin Stem.
Bowl and Foot Clear Crystal—Not Optic

TIFFIN

15078. 9 oz.
Goblet

15078. 5½ oz.
Champagne

15078. 5½ oz.
Saucer Champagne

15078. 4 oz.
Claret

15078. 3½ oz.
Large Wine

15078. 2½ oz.
Small Wine

15078. 3 oz.
Cocktail

15078. 1¼ oz.
Large Cordial

15078. 1 oz.
Small Cordial

R 15079 Line, Colored.   Amber, Green or Royal Blue Stem and Foot
with Crystal Bowl—Not Optic

15079. 9 oz.
Goblet

15079. 5½ oz.
Saucer Champagne

15079. 5½ oz.
Sundae

15079. 5½ oz.
Cafe Parfait

15079. 5 oz.
Champagne

15079. 2½ oz.
Wine

15079. 3½ oz.
Cocktail

15079. 2 oz.
Sherry

15079. 1 oz.
Cordial

15079. 1 oz.
Pousse Cafe

15079. 2¼ oz.
Whiskey, Ftd.

15079. 4½ oz.
Seltzer, Ftd.

15079. 9½ oz.
Table, Ftd.

15079. 12½ oz.
Iced Tea, Ftd.

Made in U. S. A.   300-4-6-34   Plate 390

Both stemlines included on this April 6, 1934, United States Glass Company catalog page
are previously undocumented Factory R lines.

Crystal with Royal Blue trim: #9738, 24 oz. Parade Decanter, faceted stopper; #15078, Wines, Fuchsia etching. $225-275, $275-325 each

Crystal with Reflex Green trim #15078, Wine, Saucer Champagne. $200-250 each

Bottom center: Crystal Goblets, Wide Optic, unknown line number. $125-175 each

Bottom right: Rose Pink with Crystal trim #15078, Perfume with the bowl cut down. The perfumes are only known in Rose Pink and were made to receive an atomizer. $100-125

Chapter 9: Bottles, Decanters, and Jugs

The United States Glass Company catalog pages included in this chapter document previously unknown bar bottles, individual decanters, water bottles and bitter bottles.

Center: Crystal #14185, 31 oz. Cocktail Shaker and metal cap, unknown engraving. $65-85

Right: April 6, 1934, United States Glass Company catalog page illustrating the #9738 and the #14185 handled decanters. The #9738 decanter was marketed as the Parade decanter. The #14185 decanter is usually found without a handle.

Below: *China, Glass, and Lamps,* April 27, 1925.

A New All-Glass Cocktail Shaker

A NEW All-Glass Cocktail Shaker destined to win laurels wherever it goes. The elimination of all metal parts reduces the cost very considerably and makes it easier to clean. No parts to tarnish. Has a strainer in the cap. All joints carefully ground to a tight fit. Finished in amber glass, and can be supplied with tumblers to match.

Prices on quantities on request.

UNITED STATES GLASS COMPANY
PITTSBURGH, PENNA.

OFFICES IN ALL PRINCIPAL CITIES

*Visit Our New Display and Sales Rooms—
Pottery & Glass Bldg., 954 Liberty Avenue,
Pittsburgh, Pa.*

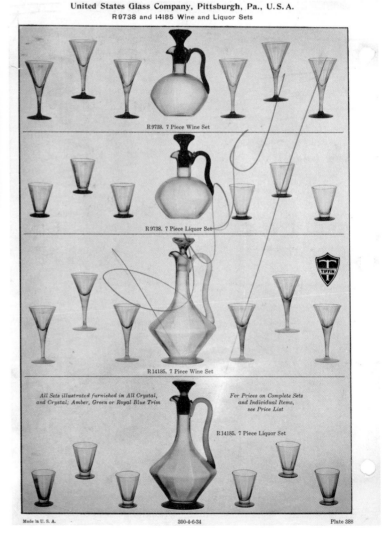

United States Glass Company, Pittsburgh, Pa., U.S.A.
R9738 and 14185 Wine and Liquor Sets

R 9738, 7 Piece Wine Set

R 9738, 7 Piece Liquor Set

R 14185, 7 Piece Wine Set

All Sets illustrated furnished in All Crystal, and Crystal; Amber, Green or Royal Blue Trim

For Prices on Complete Sets and Individual Items, see Price List

R 14185, 7 Piece Liquor Set

Made in U.S.A.   300-4-6-34   Plate 388

Top left: Crystal with Royal Blue trim: #14185, Cocktails, Wide Optic; #9738, 24 oz. Parade Decanter, faceted stopper. $15-25 each, $125-150

Top right: Crystal with Reflex Green trim #14185, Cocktails, Decanter, faceted stopper, both Wide Optic. $15-25 each, $200-250

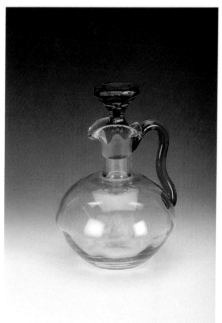

Crystal with Amber trim #9738, 24 oz. Parade Decanter, faceted stopper. $75-100

Canary: #354, 12 oz. Tumblers; #6461, 2 qt. Covered Jug, Wide Optic. $20-30 each, $175-225

Crystal with Amber trim #15012, 2 qt. Jug; Amber #15012, 1/2 lb. Candy Jar with cover. Both Wide Optic. $175-225, $50-75

Top: Crystal with Amber trim: #15003, Jug; #15003, Wine, Goblet, both with cased "buttons;" #15003, Jug with cover. All items Spiral Optic. Note that the jug on the left is not made to receive a lid. $175-225, $35-45, $35-45, $200-250
Bottom: Crystal with Amber trim: #14194, 2 qt. Jug with cover; #14199, Sundae, 10 oz. Goblet. Both Block Optic. $200-250, $15-25, $20-30

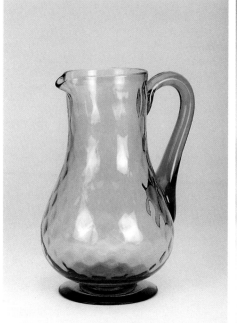

Top left: Rose Pink: #9712, 2 qt. Jug; #14194, 2 qt. Jug. Both Wide Optic. $175-225 each
Bottom left: Twilite #9712, 2 qt. Jug, Diamond Optic. $250-300
Bottom center: Crystal with Lilac trim #15001, Wine; Lilac with Crystal trim #15012, 2 qt. Jug. Both Wide Optic. $20-30, $200-250

Ruby with Crystal trim #14194, 2 qt. Jug. $350-425

A *"Several Purpose"* Beverage Set

NUMBER

6450

LIGHT GREEN

OPTIC

1 No. 6450 Jug (2-qt.)

1 No. 9353 Reamer

6 No. 444 Tumblers (12-oz.)

Packs 1 Doz. Sets to Standard Bbl. Weight 125 lbs.

A "taking" novelty in household glassware, and one which has many uses. Lemonade or other fruit-juice beverages can be prepared with minimum effort and, without the Reamer, the set is just right for ice water or iced tea.

UNITED STATES GLASS COMPANY

PITTSBURGH, PA.

COMBINATION
Iced Tea and Reamer Set
No. 6450
(Pat. applied for)

ICE TUB No. 8129

SET No. 6475

SET No. 617

SET No. 185

SET No. 194

The NEWEST
in beverage sets
and one for every purse ~

COMBINATION Iced Tea and Reamer Set No. 6450 and our new line of table-size ICE TUBS are sweeping aside the old idea of waiting for the sweltering July days to stimulate sales of Beverage Sets. These items are in steady demand—NOW—every month in the year.

You will profit most from the increased year-round use of Beverage Sets by featuring No. 6450 with the popular Ice Tubs and by displaying a sufficient variety of sets to enable your customers to have a choice.

Both Set No. 6450 and Ice Tub No. 8129 are furnished in rose-pink and apple-green glass to match. All other sets illustrated above are available in rose-pink and crystal with green or amber trim.

Combination Iced Tea and Reamer Sets are sold only by us. Order a stock today—Everything you'll need in Beverage Sets.

UNITED STATES GLASS COMPANY
World's Largest Makers of Household Glassware.
PITTSBURGH, PA.
Sales Offices in All Principal Cities.

Top left: *China, Glass, and Lamps,* April 4, 1927.

Top right: *China, Glass, and Lamps,* May 9, 1927.

Bottom left: *China, Glass, and Lamps,* May 9, 1927.

Bottom right: *China, Glass, and Lamps.*

Added Features Help Beverage Set Sales

THERE is no mystery in the growing year 'round use of refreshment sets in the home. Wise ones click their tongues and, with a knowing smile, say, "Ah. Yes."—but there is really a bigger reason and one that the United States Glass Co. is taking advantage of, to the profit of itself and its dealers right now.

That reason is the mounting popularity and widespread use of iceless refrigeration. The lowly cake of ice is becoming almost a piece-de-resistance, both in homes where the ice-man makes his daily rounds and those where the little tray of sparkling ice cubes makes its welcome appearance at mealtimes and in between. The latest are colored cubes, flavored with grape juice and other palatable syrups.

It is no wonder that iceless refrigeration has made ice, and iced drinks, popular for daily table use—not ordinary iced-water, but flavored drinks that are building a big demand for the United States Glass Co.'s new and patented combination iced tea and reamer set No. 6450, pictured herewith, as well as for the new and handy table-size ice tubs.

How handy it is to have a jug with a seed-catching reamer that fits into the top and never gets lost. Because U. S. G. Co. ice-tubes are finding as great favor as the combination iced tea and reamer sets, it has become almost a slogan with the United States Glass Co. to "Sell an Ice-Tub with every Beverage Set."

The line of beverage sets which the United States Glass Co. is offering the trade this year is wide in variety and color combinations—a revelation in artistry and good taste.

All of which emphasizes the fact that dealers who have

adopted the suggestions of the United States Glass Co. have learned that it is not necessary to wait for the sweltering July days to sell beverage sets.

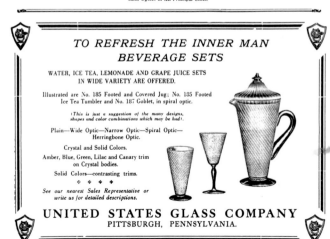

TO REFRESH THE INNER MAN
BEVERAGE SETS

WATER, ICE TEA, LEMONADE AND GRAPE JUICE SETS
IN WIDE VARIETY ARE OFFERED.

Illustrated are No. 185 Footed and Covered Jug; No. 185 Footed
Ice Tea Tumbler and No. 187 Goblet, in spiral optic.

*(This is just a suggestion of the many designs,
shapes and color combinations which may be had).*

Plain—Wide Optic—Narrow Optic—Spiral Optic—
Herringbone Optic.

Crystal and Solid Colors.

Amber, Blue, Green, Lilac and Canary trim
on Crystal bodies.

Solid Colors—contrasting trims.

See our nearest Sales Representative or
write us for detailed descriptions.

UNITED STATES GLASS COMPANY
PITTSBURGH, PENNSYLVANIA.

Top left: April, 1924, *The Glass Outlook*, a United States Glass Company publication.

Top right: *China, Glass, and Lamps*, March, 1924, advertisement. Note that the lid was formed to cover the spout.

Bottom left: *China, Glass, and Lamps*, February 21, 1927.

Bottom right: *China, Glass, and Lamps*, September, 1929.

Gold Encrusted Glassware

LASTING beauty—beauty of line and decoration—is the dominant note in the appeal of these gold encrusted pieces. Fine lead blown glass that rings clear and true as a bell is the foundation. Eighteen carat gold in plain bands and Leaf, Laurel, and Minton designs are the decorations. Ask for complete illustrations and prices.

Look for the Banner Gold Label on every piece of United States Quality Glassware.

UNITED STATES GLASS CO., PITTSBURGH, PA.

13

Glassware for Summer

What could be finer for a cooling draught on the porch or in the sun parlor? The dainty green jug and tumbler here illustrated breathes an air of refinement and summer comfort. United States decorated glass is available in a variety of pieces.

This illustration shows No. 6455 Green Jug and Cover and No. 444, 10-oz. Tumbler—Cut 119.

UNITED STATES GLASS COMPANY
General Offices and Salesrooms
South Ninth and Bingham Sts. Pittsburgh, Pa.

New York: 1107 Broadway, E. T. W. Craig, Representative
Philadelphia: 10th and Market Sts. J. A. Hemple, Representative
San Francisco: 682 Mission Street, F. M. Dunn, Representative

Boston: 99 Bedford Street, M. A. Lovell, Representative
Los Angeles: 643 South Olive Street, J. F. Stirk, Representative
Dallas: Southland Hotel Building, D. D. Otstott, Inc., Representative
St. Louis: 1017 Olive St., J. Donald Fisher, Representative.

Baltimore: 110 Hopkins Place, John A. Dobson Co., Representative
Chicago: 30 East Randolph Street, F. T. Renshaw, Representative
Denver, 404 Jacobson Building, Norton C. Boyer, Representative.

UNITED STATES WARES GIVE COMPLETE SERVICE

Rock Crystal Cutting No. 413.

From the finest in lead blown glassware in quality cuttings, including Rock Crystal, to unique and unusual wares for every-day service, our lines are complete.

The No. 413 Rock Crystal Cutting from our Tiffin factory is NEW and is on a NEW shape. It will prove a big retailer. Our Tiffin line includes many other wares of equal quality. Tableware is available to complement stemware in shape and decoration. Colors and combinations, too.

New wares for the Holiday also are offered in pressed and blown wares. These include gift specialties and exclusive utility wares for the home.

Ample facilities and better service than ever before.

New Cocktail Set, Patents Applied For

UNITED STATES GLASS COMPANY
PITTSBURGH
Sales Offices in All Principal Cities.

Only a few Months, and
Summer Will Arrive—

No. 6471 OPTIC ICED TEA SET

When the buying public will need Beverage Sets in large quantities. The set illustrated consists of 1 12 doz. No. 6471 Optic Covered Jug and one-half doz. No. 444 Optic 12 oz. Tumblers, designed for Iced Tea service. The same Jug, with or without cover, can be assembled into sets with smaller matching Tumblers, for service of other beverages, such as Lemonade, Grape Juice, etc.

Listed in the new and popular shades of light green and rose-pink, and at prices which will enable the jobber or dealer to move this number in volume. For detailed information, write direct or to any of our eighteen sales offices, conveniently located in principal cities of the United States and Canada.

UNITED STATES GLASS COMPANY
PITTSBURGH, PA.

Chapter 10: Additional Tableware

Many of these tableware items are documented here for the first time. Plate etchings, engravings, or colored trim were used to decorate finger bowls, hollow stem champagnes, cocktail shakers, grape fruits, salt shakers, cruets and ice tubs.

Excerpt from mid 1930s United States Glass Company catalog. Line numbers with an R prefix are Factory R products; line numbers with a G prefix are Factory G (Glassport, PA) products.

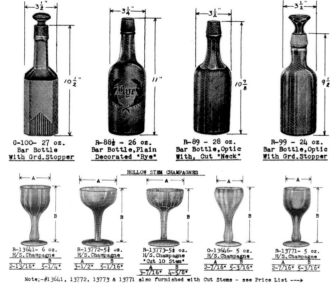

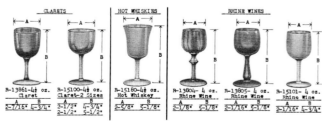

Excerpts from mid 1930s United States Glass Company catalog.

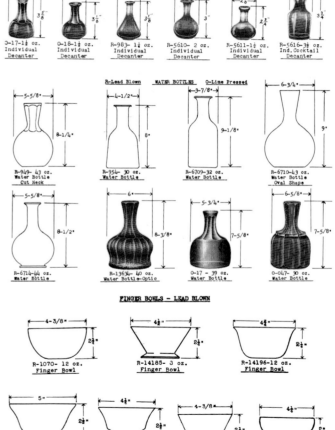

Excerpts from mid 1930s United States Glass Company catalog. Line numbers with an O prefix are Factory O (Central Glass Company), Wheeling, West Virginia.

Excerpts from mid 1930s United States Glass Company catalog.

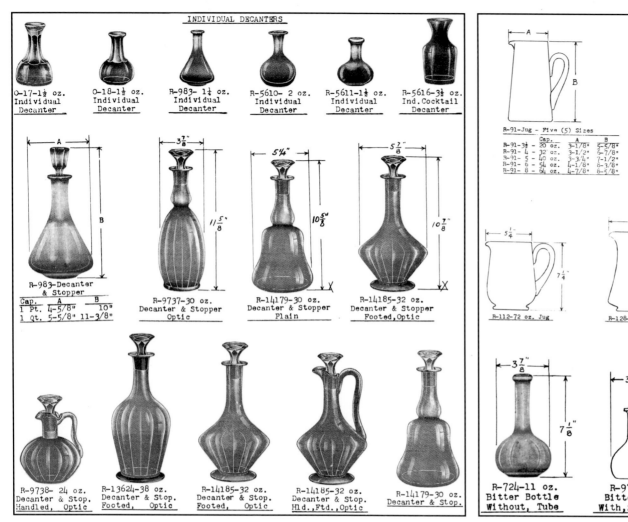

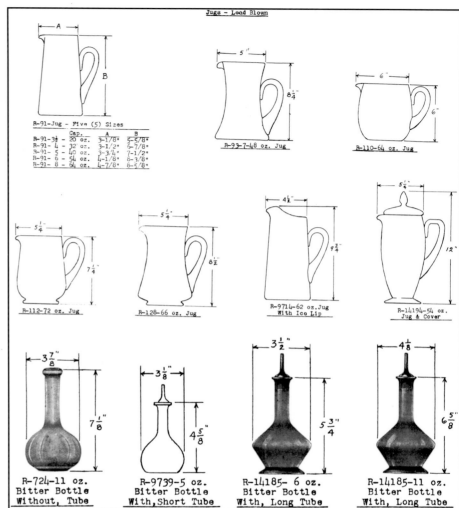

Excerpts from mid 1930s United States Glass
Company catalog.

Excerpts from mid 1930s United States Glass
Company catalog.

172

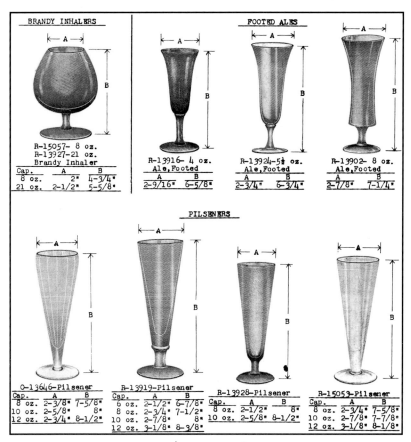

Excerpts from mid 1930s United States Glass Company catalog.

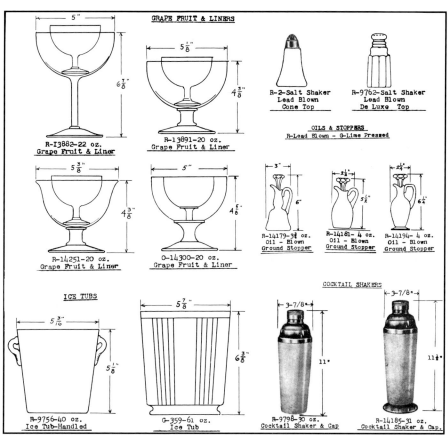

Excerpts from mid 1930s United States Glass Company catalog.

173

Tiffin Glass Collectors Club

The Tiffin Glass Collectors Club is a non-profit corporation with tax exempt status, which was established in 1985 to study the history of Tiffin Glass, known as Factory R of the United States Glass Company, and the glassware manufactured there.

Membership in the club includes collectors from all over the United States. A club newsletter is published quarterly for members, and features minutes, glass articles, and historical data, and other information of interest to collectors.

Activities of the Tiffin Glass Collectors Club include the glass shows held in June and November and fund-raisers which benefit the Archive Foundation and a future Tiffin Glass Museum.

For more information, inquiries may be directed to the Tiffin Glass Collectors Club, P.O. Box 554, Tiffin, Ohio 44883.

Sources

In addition to private archival documents, information for this book was taken from the following sources:

Bickenheuser, Fred; *Tiffin Glassmasters*, Book I. Grove City, Ohio Glassmasters Publications, 1979.

Bickenheuser, Fred; *Tiffin Glassmasters*, Book II. Grove City, Ohio Glassmasters Publications, 1981.

Page, Bob and Frederiksen, Dale; *Tiffin is Forever*. Greensboro, North Carolina: Page-Frederiksen Publishing Co., 1994.

China, Glass, and Lamps.

United States Glass Company Catalogs: 1913, 1919, 1924, 1934, 1935, 1936, 1937, and assorted 1920s Catalog Pages.

United States Glass Company Price Lists: 1920, 1921, 1924.

Tiffin Glass Collectors Club: Tiffin Glassmasters newsletters.

Index